WINTER'S LIGHT

John Preston

WINTER'S LIGHT

REFLECTIONS OF A

YANKEE QUEER

Edited and with an Introduction by Michael Lowenthal

Foreword by Andrew Holleran

University Press of New England
Hanover and London

University Press of New England, Hanover, NH 03755
© 1995 by the Estate of John Preston.
Introduction and notes © 1995 by Michael Lowenthal.
Foreword © 1995 by Andrew Holleran.
All rights reserved
Printed in the United States of America
5 4 3 2 1
CIP data appear at the end of the book

CONTENTS

Some of Us Are Dying

A New England Chorus

Down East

A C K N O W L E D G M E N T S

Given John Preston's emphasis on the value of community, it seems especially appropriate to acknowledge the community of individuals who helped me complete this, his final book.

I feel privileged to have met so many friends in John's adopted town of Portland, particularly Agnes Bushell and Tom Hagerty. It has also been a joy to become close to John's mother Nancy, sister Betsy, and brother Marvin, who have been generous in sharing their son and brother.

For their helpful comments on the manuscript, I want to acknowledge Agnes Bushell, Andrew Holleran, Michael Rowe, and especially Susan Ackerman. Thanks also to my colleagues at University Press of New England, who supported the project from its inception, and to Chris Hogan, who sustained me in the difficult time of John's illness.

Finally, my greatest appreciation goes to John Preston, who showed me an example of a model Yankee and a model queer, and that it was possible to be both at once.

M. L.

FOREWORD

I met John Preston only three times. I knew him chiefly through our correspondence. Our letters went up and down the eastern seaboard, from north Florida, where I live, to Portland, Maine. Both of us were gay men who had lived in New York, but were now in much quieter places; both of us writers who loved news about other writers and books; both of us people for whom the day's harvest at the post office was the focal point of the day. Then, too, there was some odd similarity between Florida and Maine—two sides of the same coin, two states at either end of the United States where people went to get away from everything in between. We telephoned only when necessary; when I did, I enjoyed not only hearing his voice, but knowing that he in his room (which I know had a hibiscus) and I in mine were two versions of a common solitude.

Pen pals are a peculiar thing—actually meeting one another can alter, if not threaten, the intimacy of the correspondence. I'd heard of John before we began corresponding; living in New York in the seventies, I'd seen a friend, the writer George Whitmore, fall under the spell of Preston's cult novel *Mr. Benson*, and watched that highest form of praise a writer can receive—T-shirts—begin to sprout in the West Village with the words LOOKING FOR MR. BENSON on them. By the time I met John, however, he was in his anthology period—reading for the Book of the Month Club, cultivating mainstream publishing contacts, selling collections of essays by gay men about where they lived (*Hometowns*) and what they thought of AIDS (*Personal Dispatches*), and getting his contributors gigs at the Miami Book Fair, among other places, to promote the books.

Preston loved going to Miami (where I met him twice) in the dead of winter, even if, as he says in the collection you are about to read, winter was his favorite season in Maine. He seemed in full bloom in Miami—the editor who had brought his friends together (writers and protégés) on the beach or in the hotels he loved: a magician of sorts.

The third time we met, however, was perhaps more characteristic: He came south on his own to give a lecture in Tallahassee, rented a car, and drove down from Savannah, Georgia. The town I live in lies between these two points. But when John called the day I expected to hear from him, he said he was in Gainesville, twenty-three miles west, and it was there we shared a lunch in an outdoor piazza on the University of Florida campus. Not one to tell people what their itinerary should be, I accepted the fact that Preston had wanted to stop off in Gainesville and see the campus there; what shocked me, however, was that halfway through his lunch he mentioned the fact that he had driven through my town on his way to Gainesville. "And you didn't call me?" I asked. He shook his head; I cannot remember his excuse, but afterwards it didn't matter—John had not come to see me in my house, had driven right past my street, I surmise, through some pen pal's sense that as intimate as we were in our letters, he was not about to bother me in my own home.

That unique combination—of intimacy and reserve—characterizes, it seems to me, the collection you are about to read. It was the essence of Preston; or the Preston I knew. The Preston I knew wrote wonderfully chatty, dish-filled letters—about his trips (to promote his books, in cities across the country; to have his blood work done, in Boston), news from publishing, the book projects he was hatching, the deadlines he met, the speeches he gave, his brother the ex-Marine, New Yorkers we knew in common, others in the menage he'd formed in Portland whom I'd never met, his dog Vlad (the Impaler), his frequent flyer programs, hotels (and, most important, *tea* at those hotels), his new car. We even, after John sent me some pages from *Consumer Reports*, bought our cars together. It's a testimony to the respect I felt for his judgment that I chose the model I got after learning that John was getting one too. I asked John advice on many matters, from writing, to aging, to sex. He always came back with concrete advice (from "Don't dye your hair!" to "Get a frequent flyer card *now!*"). He was interested in everything and knew, moreover, exactly what he felt about it.

These qualities flavor the pieces gathered together by Michael Lowenthal for this collection. But most of it is new to me. For one, the depth of John's identification with his home—with Portland, Maine, which as he says in the opening evocation of his hometown, turned out to be a place people who had grown up in Massachusetts went when they wished to find the things they had loved in childhood. If all politics is local, then all literature is too, and nothing illustrates that better than this book. Preston zeroes in on the gay, and human, dilemma: How to find a home. The opening essay—his paean to Medfield, Massachusetts—gives a clue to the firm sense of self that enabled Preston to live the openly gay life that he did in Maine, and also the dilemma ("I was being taken away from Medfield and everything it stood for," he writes, when he realized he was gay) and the anger this dilemma engendered: Why should he have to leave Medfield in the first place?

There was, and probably still is, no answer to that. So Preston left; staying just a year in various cities, because, as he puts it, at that point in his life, "Having a hometown wasn't the point. Being gay was our geographic location." Which makes it all the more affecting to read in this book of his decision, finally, to weld together the two elements of his identity (geography and sexual preference; home and homosexuality) by moving to Portland and refusing to pretend. In Portland, by taking an open and public place as a gay writer/activist/spokesman, he and others who were "willing to be interviewed," he writes, ". . . began to give Portland and its lesbian and gay life a human face."

Very human. The pride he took in being one of the guys at his barbershop—the Greek chorus to his life; his honest account of his fantasy ("A Minister Calls") of gaining access to the pulpits of leading New England churches; his chilling interview with Bob Gravel (a story that would not surprise Nathaniel Hawthorne); show John standing somewhere between the grim reality of the Gravel case (and the Charlie Howard murder) and the romantic, wistful idealism of "Down East"— that perfect place even residents of Maine know will probably never be found. Obviously Preston both loved New England and had no illusions about it.

This strength of mind is equally evident in his writings and speeches on the subject of AIDS, the disease that shortened his tenure in the home he'd made for himself. Preston in his letters never complained about his HIV infection. He mentioned his trips to doctors in Boston, the drug trials he was in or trying to get in, the pneumonia (described with remorseless exactitude in "Living with AIDS, 1992"), even the onset of his final illness, but he never let them alter the pleasure and interest in life that emanated from all his correspondence. The last letter simply said: "Please keep your end up, even if I can't."

It was like dropping a letter down a deep, dark well, as the weeks went on without a reply from Preston (whose letters, I learned early on, were interrupted by only two things: extended travel, and illness). When the phone call came from one of his innumerable friends—in this case, an erstwhile dominatrix who is now a minister working in Manhattan hospitals—it was no surprise. Still, it caused a unique void. The only compensation for never getting another letter from John could be this posthumous book in which—though he could not live to put the pieces together himself—one gets the essential Preston very clearly.

September 1994   ANDREW HOLLERAN

INTRODUCTION

John Preston was a fabricator. He liked to make things up.

This was a useful predilection for a man who made most of his living writing novels and stories. Author of the cult classic *Mr. Benson*, among numerous other pornographic tales, and of the *Black Beret* and *Mission of Alex Kane* action/adventure series, he had, to say the least, an extremely active fantasy life. Between 1983 and 1993, by himself or with a collaborator, he cranked out some thirty books of fiction.

But John was not only a writer of sexual fantasies and action/adventure pulp. He was a journalist, an essayist, and an expert compiler of anthologies who published in *Harper's* and produced two Book of the Month Club selections. He wrote serious nonfiction about the pressing personal and political issues he faced as a gay man in our society.

On the whole, John's breadth of expertise and range of talent were extremely advantageous. The diversity of his work allowed him always to have a dozen or so projects going at once. This was how he cultivated such a wide network of professional acquaintances and how he managed to make a living as a freelancer. If the novel about cult prostitutes in the ancient Near East wasn't sparking his imagination at a given moment, he could grab the next pile on his desk: an article on the state of AIDS research, or an anthology about the families gay men create.

But there was a problem. Sometimes John's fantasies crept into his nonfiction work. He so liked to tell tales, and had such a vivid sense of what *should* happen in any given story, that occasionally he couldn't help but tinker with the events of real life.

One of John's set pieces that seemed likely a stretch of the truth was his series of anecdotes about the people of Portland, Maine, his adopted hometown. John had moved there in 1979 after living for at least a year in each of a succession of major urban centers: Chicago, Minneapolis, San Francisco, Los Angeles, Philadelphia, and New York. Though not exactly where he'd grown up—that was some two hours' drive south, in a small town in Massachusetts—Portland felt like a homecoming nonetheless. John reveled in the familiar accents, the seasons that changed at the appropriate times. John accepted himself as a New Englander. This was where he belonged.

But did the New Englanders accept him? Did they feel he belonged? Could a gay man gain full membership in their community?

These were the questions that haunted John, and he scrutinized his life to find evidence that the answer was yes. John recounted numerous incidents, in his writing and in his conversations, about how much a part of the Portland community he was. He wrote with pride of the men at the corner barbershop and how they defended him when homophobic remarks were overheard. He spoke of being welcomed by name at Joe's Smoke Shop, where they knew just what he'd buy when he walked in. Even the bag boys at the supermarket were said to recognize him.

I had lived in small-town New England myself for some eight years (real small-town New England, not Portland, a city with a metropolitan population of some 200,000), and I had not experienced the degree of neighborly acceptance John described. Sure, one of the half dozen postal clerks had learned my first name. I exchanged friendly glances with some familiar faces when we passed one another on the town green. But nothing on the level John claimed. I began to wonder if his anecdotes were more wishful thinking than reality.

In late 1993 and early 1994, when John became incapacitated by AIDS, I began visiting him once a week to help care for him and keep his business in order. I had never been to

Portland before. My friendship with John had been one based on daily phone conversations, frequent letters, and occasional meetings in Boston and other neutral territories.

On one of my first visits, the person who'd volunteered to walk John's dog Vlad the Impaler had to cancel (John was too sick to leave the house), so I stepped in. I followed John's directions to the cemetery and when I got there, I let Vlad run free among the gravestones. A few minutes later, a stranger walked up to me and asked, "How's John feeling today?" Startled, I answered with a nervous "Not too great, but okay," and thanked her for her concern. The woman walked away, but a few minutes later another stranger approached and asked the same question. By the time Vlad had finished his business, two more people had inquired about John's health. None of them had seen me before, but they recognized Vlad and knew John's affairs intimately enough to conclude I must be taking care of him.

A few visits later, I was pulling together a publicity mailing for John's latest book, *My Life as a Pornographer and Other Indecent Acts*. John had experienced a very bad period during which he was hardly able to sit up for a few days. But now he had regained enough energy that he asked if he could help with the mailing. I assigned him the job of writing his return address in the upper left corner of some of the envelopes, which he did in his characteristic shorthand: "Box 5314, Ptland ME 04101." He never bothered to write out his name.

When all of the envelopes had been stuffed and addressed, I took them over to the post office and presented the pile to the postal clerk. The first few envelopes happened to be ones that I'd addressed. When the clerk flipped to one with John's handwriting he stopped and said, "Well that's good. John must be feeling better today."

I was astounded. Without even the benefit of seeing John's name, this postal worker could recognize his handwriting and deduce that his health had improved from one day to the next. At that moment I realized that John's stories about his level of acceptance by the dog walkers and postal workers were not fabricated; if anything, they were understatements.

Through the course of my numerous visits to Portland during John's illness, and finally for his funeral, I saw again and again that he had indeed gained full membership in the community. From the visiting nurses, to the many volunteers who took shifts watching him, to Franny the ninety-year-old matron, to Albert the florist who delivered arrangements three times a week—most of whom had read many of John's books— the people of Portland counted John as one of their own. This was truly his hometown.

When John Preston moved from New York to Maine in 1979, his friends thought he was crazy. Contemporary gay literature as we know it was on the verge of being born in Manhattan. Andrew Holleran's *Dancer from the Dance* and Larry Kramer's *Faggots* had just been published. The Violet Quill, a group of soon-to-be-prominent gay writers including Holleran, Edmund White, Felice Picano, and others, would form there the very next year. And here was Preston, a man who was just attempting to embark on a career as a gay writer, abandoning this rich literary scene for a new home in what for gay men might as well have been the moon.

But it was precisely the development of Gay Writing as a self-conscious genre that provided much of the impetus for John's flight north. In later years he often spoke derisively about the elitism of the Violet Quill and similar "schools" of gay writing, but the truth was that these groups had scared him away. "I saw them as an enormous threat," he once commented. "My voice as a writer was so weak, and I wasn't confident of it. To put it into a writers' group terrified me."

John recognized early on that his fiction would never be *New Yorker* material and that to enter the world of High Literature and attempt to conform his voice to its dictates would mean his death as a writer. So he removed himself from this circle and went to a place where he could concentrate on building a body of work with the tools he did possess.

John was a literary equivalent of the jazz trumpeter Miles Davis, who had none of the technical prowess of trumpet players like Clifford Brown or Dizzy Gillespie, but whose innate sense of the music was unarguably masterful. Like Davis, who developed a trademark style in which the silences between notes were as important as the notes themselves, John created a bare-bones writing style that he tried to make as muscularly raw as the men who loaded ships at the docks of Portland's waterfront. Instead of literary fanfares and flourishes, John came to rely on his gut sense of his audience, his almost primal identification with other gay men.

It worked. By moving away from the fast track, John was able to connect with something that other gay writers were missing. "Moving to Maine really helped me clarify my use of symbols," he reflected in the last interview he ever gave. "The original gay writers—myself included—would write things assuming that no gay man knew how to fix a car. That we were aesthetes of some sort. I moved to Maine, and the first thing I realized was—they *do*. The gay men of Maine know how to fix a car!"

John thrived on immersion in his audience, and he used the members of his new community in Portland as litmus tests for the work he was producing. He commented, "I don't let anything go out that my next-door neighbor Greg, who's a gay man from Maine, wouldn't understand. So I'm not self-defined by the gay ghetto, which I think has made a huge difference in my life."

John's discovery, or rediscovery, of a home outside of the urban gay centers was not an easy process. "I had to leave my family to be gay," he began one of his best-known essays, and it was the pain of this exile from family, home, and community that inspired much of his gay activism as well as his writing.

He wrote eloquently of the gay man's dilemma in his introduction to *Hometowns: Gay Men Write about Where They Belong*, the anthology he edited as a way of working through these issues:

> Where we come from is important to who we are. . . . Do we sense that we fit? Do we feel welcome? Do we experience ourselves as valued members of the community? How are we perceived by our neighbors and peers? These are among the most fundamental questions we have to answer.
>
> Most men begin with the promise that we are, in fact, welcome. The boy child is, in almost all our known contexts, the heir. He has a right to assume that he will acquire whatever is possible in his world. If his background includes being the member of a disenfranchised group because of race, religion, ethnic background, or class status, he still has the expectation of achieving the most that background will give him.
>
> The gay man, since he is primarily a man, begins with those assumptions. It isn't until he comes of age and understands his sexual identity and the way it separates him from his birth community that a gay man achieves a perception of being a member of this particular minority. . . .
>
> One of the first questions that a gay man has to answer revolves around the basic issue: Where do I belong? Having grown up as a privileged member of his community, he will now have to ask himself if he can stay there. For years, gay men thought they only had two choices: They could either sublimate their erotic identities and remain in their hometown, or they could move to large centers of population and lose themselves in anonymity. There was no way for a gay man to have a hometown and still be honest with himself. He had to hide his social and sexual proclivities, or else he had to give up communal life in pursuit of them.

John's move to Portland was in large part an effort to create more options for gay men, to prove by sheer force of will that it was indeed possible to be happily and openly gay—and at the same time a member of a community—outside of the ghetto. He considered the mere fact of his choosing to live in Portland, particularly in the early years, as a show of activism.

But for all of John's political theorizing about the necessity of community and the imperative that gay men be able to return home, his obsession with Portland was really a reflection of his own personal and psychological needs. John cultivated an image as the self-made man, the renegade, but he knew more than anybody that, without the company of others, he was lost. He had not chosen expulsion. He had not chosen the years of wandering. The life of independence had been forced on him and had caused him great pain.

At John's funeral, his longtime friend and editor Michael Denneny commented:

> It strikes me as ironic that this man who, in the seventies, had an almost legendary reputation as a literary and erotic outlaw— and that in a community itself virtually outlawed—that this man's central theme, in both his life and his writings, was community. . . . He was one of the few people I have known for whom the need for community was an immediate and tangible reality. He spent years moving from city to city until he realized that at heart he was a New Englander and he came to Portland, to be near to his roots and his family.

Sexually and politically, John was indeed a radical in many ways. But his radicalness was not in his rejection of norms, it was in his embrace of them. To demonstrate proudly his identity as a gay man, but at the same time to seek—no, demand— membership in a hometown community, was his truly renegade action.

"In some essential way," John told an interviewer, "life outside New England has never made any sense to me."

In his last few years, John sought to immerse himself deeper and deeper into the culture and traditions of New England. He read regional histories and biographies of important New England personalities. He asked me to bring him books on the Puritans and a copy of the Mayflower Compact. It was all the background against which he was going to tell the story of his own life.

John was thrilled to receive a contract from University Press of New England for *Winter's Light: Reflections of a Yankee Queer*. The advance payment he received was less than a tenth of what he had received for previous books, but that didn't matter. He felt a profound sense of rightness that his book would be published by a house with "New England" right there in its name. And an academic publisher—no small feat for the world's most prominent gay pornographer. After leaving his boyhood home in Massachusetts, after being told in college that he would never be an English major because his accent was wrong, after turning his back on New York and its gay literary scene, John was finally being recognized by the community that meant the most to him.

John viewed *Winter's Light* as a perfect opportunity to explore the specific and, by doing so, make it universal. The volume would be at once a book about the uniqueness of gay life in New England and about the common need for gay men to reconcile their various identities.

It was with a deep sense of sadness that John realized he would never finish this book. He had planned to write more essays exploring his ever-increasing understanding of New England and its influences on him. He had mapped out pieces about the recent referendum on Portland's ban on antigay discrimination, about listening to Boston Red Sox games with his favorite bachelor uncle, and other subjects.

But John had already written the core of his book. The crucial elements are all represented: his Massachusetts boyhood, his wandering and eventual return to New England, his participation in the creation of a gay life in Maine, his insistence on communal responsibility in the face of AIDS. The work included here stands as a record of his lifelong struggle, finally successful, to find community.

For John, living this struggle was not enough. He had to write about it, to share the experience with others, so that those who followed would have an easier journey along the path. When he wrote the proposal for what would eventually become this volume, John sketched out a preliminary introduction. The last paragraphs of that sketch serve fittingly here as his statement of intent. The work in this book, he wrote, is

> based on the assumption that it is necessary to write about our lives in order to save them. I have lived with the silence of gay life before Stonewall, and I know how deadly it can be. I certainly know how deadly silence about AIDS can be.
>
> This book is many things for me. It is a compilation of my observations about what has happened to us all in the last ten years. It is a statement of defiance about the way that we have been treated in the past. It is an expression of hope in the future, especially of hope in the way that writing can be a statement that people existed, struggled, won victories and suffered defeat.
>
> These are human stories that have taken place while I was trying to save my own life.

Boston, Massachusetts   MICHAEL LOWENTHAL
September 1994

THE IMPORTANCE OF
TELLING OUR STORIES

The title of the opening essay speaks for itself. Preston had un-wavering faith that to tell his story, to name himself and his life in words, was an act of irrevocable affirmation. Here he tells of his place in his family's long New England legacy, of his boyhood in Massachusetts, and of his eventual return to New England. Thus is the frame of his journey set.

The Importance of Telling Our Stories

When I was young I asked my father where I had come from. He's an engineer, and he believes that all knowledge derives from facts. Following his scientific instinct, he sat me down and drew diagrams of sperm cells and ovaries, explaining in technical detail the physiology of how life begins.

I was embarrassed. Not by his explanation—I knew all that—but because he had so badly misunderstood my question.

So I went to my mother and asked her where I had come from. She was in her chair reading. She put down her book and nodded her head slightly, just enough to let me know that this was an important question. Then she launched into a long, complex answer that began with my great-great-grandfather and his brother, who had left the Green Mountains of Vermont in search of their fortune, endured a few false starts in various villages, and eventually settled in our hometown of Medfield, Massachusetts.

We had lived there ever since, my mother explained. Anyone who married into our family moved to Medfield and settled there to raise their children, just as my father had moved to our rural community from his home in Boston after he and my mother were married. This was where I belonged, she explained, because this is where I came from.

My mother's answer was exactly what I had been looking for. It was all the more appealing because the story was full of small details that brought to life the people in my history. The ancient New England names were the richest part. The founding patriarch, my great-great-grandfather, was Raymond Blood, and his name had appeared in every generation since.

Now I understood how my uncle came to be called Raymond. My mother's father had been a Raymond Blood as well. And just to underscore how lavish that name was, he married a woman named Martha Honey. Blood and honey—how much more elemental can a boy's heritage be?

The part of the story that interested me most was my ancestors' journey from Vermont. I imagined the original Raymond Blood and his brother riding huge horse-drawn wagons down from the mountains. My mother had told me the brothers were always said to have been extremely close to each other; I could sense the fraternity between them as they camped under tarps while they built the first family house in Medfield. It was over on Park Street, my mother said.

The whole landscape of my childhood became alive with possibilities after I heard this story. I began to ask questions about the old landmarks in our hometown, wanting to know just what things would have looked like when my ancestors first arrived in Medfield. As soon as I was old enough, I read town histories, knowing that this history was meant for me. This was history that my family had made me a part of over the course of the past two centuries.

When I was older, I entered another world where there were few stories to give me that same sense of fitting in. This was the world of bus stations and hotel rooms, of men having sex with men, and sometimes loving one another. There were no histories of this life. I did read some psychological texts about homosexuality, but they were mainly about the dysfunction and deviance of a homosexual lifestyle. Their cold analysis was of as little help to me as my father's technical diagrams of sperms cells and eggs.

How could I create a life on that basis? I was *sure* there was something more to my sexual orientation than statistical tables. But where was it all?

It was the fifties and television certainly wasn't acknowledging homosexual lifestyles. The newspapers told of no political groups advocating for our civil rights. Magazines never carried any material about the lifestyle I was about to enter aside from the occasional veiled innuendo of a terrible scandal. The person I was becoming was invisible to the world—and almost invisible to me. That's why I, like so many other young people at the time, thought I must be the only person in the world who experienced these feelings. If there were others, wouldn't they be reported somewhere? Wouldn't their existence be recognized by someone?

I finally found a very few pieces of writing that hinted at another level of richness. I read avant-garde literary magazines and books, hungry for their portrayals of what it might be like to be a homosexual. But tales of urban adventure such as John Rechy's *City of Night* didn't really fulfill my needs either. After all, I was a kid in a small rural town, doing well in school, expected to go to college. I wasn't living on the cutting edge of society, I was smack dab in the middle of it. How would this new intelligence about dropouts, addicts, and perverts fit into my life?

While I was in high school and later in college, I discovered a magic place—Provincetown, Massachusetts—that started to give me the solutions I craved. Provincetown is an old beach resort at the very tip of Cape Cod. It has been an artists' colony for years, and because of its cultured reputation—and maybe because it is the very edge of the country, the end of the world—Provincetown has long been a center of homosexual life. When I first visited I saw that the town's very isolation seemed to allow the people there to construct an honest existence that nourished them. It wasn't perfect—there was no place in the United States in the fifties where being homosexual was not problematic—but it was a place where gay men and lesbians could congregate comfortably.

I started to go to Provincetown as often as I could. I went there for the bars where the men who hid when they were in Boston actually danced together and kissed in public. There was a great sexual thrill to being in Provincetown and taking part in all of its open courtship rituals. But I also went because this was one place where people were willing to tell their stories.

I would stand by the dance floor in a bar, or lie on my blanket at the gay beach at Herring Cove, and I would listen to gay men and lesbians tell one another about their lives. The narratives were often simple, about getting along with a landlord and deciding where to live, or about working in a certain place.

The stories I heard in Provincetown's restaurants and on its streets were also frequently profound. There were tales about the horrors that gay life could mean back then, being harassed and evicted, all the cruelty society could hand out to its unwanted. But there were also proposals about how to change things. Long before Stonewall and the birth of the contemporary gay rights movement, many lesbians and gay men were wondering out loud how we could create a better life for all of us.

These stories became as important to me as the stories my mother told me about my family because they too were about my heritage and my place in the world. They were all the more important because they were so scarce.

When I eventually became a gay activist, I remembered the power of stories. I was one of the founders of the first gay and lesbian community center in the United States, Gay House, Inc., in Minneapolis. One of the first things we did at Gay House was establish times when people of different types could come together and talk about their lives. We weren't trying to solve all the world's problems with our discussion groups; we were just taking advantage of a chance finally to talk to one another about those problems.

The discussion circles included many different affinity

groups. There were times when lesbian mothers could talk to one another, other times when single gay men met among themselves. Then there were larger community meetings at which everyone who used the place came together at once. We all gained different things from those meetings, but the essential benefit was learning to listen to one another and thus beginning to understand how we had gotten to this place of being lesbian and gay.

By the time I became a writer, in the late seventies, a whole body of lesbian and gay literature was beginning to become available in bookstores across the country. Where once I had found only texts on abnormal behavior and ways to curb or prevent it, there were now novels, poems, plays, and true stories about being gay and lesbian.

Not all of them told my particular story. Like those discussion groups at Gay House, some conversations were intended for only a limited circle of people and others for the entire community. And when I didn't find important legends and tales that reflected my own life, I did the same thing I had done as a community organizer: I made my own.

The first novel I wrote, *Franny, the Queen of Provincetown*, is a series of monologues by different characters. It celebrates the voices I had heard years earlier in that old resort community, the voices that had broken the silence and told me about a world of possibilities.

Many parts of *Franny* were fun to write, the charming tales of happiness and fantasy. Other parts were hard to put down on paper, painful but necessary warnings about the obstacles we faced: external restraints such as discrimination, and internal ones such as drug abuse. These elements combined to form a story that made sense to me, a story that reflected my place in the world.

I'm sure it's her own love of stories that led my mother to be extremely proud of *Franny*. About the time it was published, my mother came to Portland for a convention. I was about to go out of town, but she asked me to stop by her hotel room for a drink, so I did. Suddenly all these people started coming into the room. I didn't understand what was going on until I saw that they were all clutching little reviews of *Franny*. They had come to meet me. It was a publication party.

In another family, a successful son might have been a doctor, lawyer, or a wealthy businessman. But in our family, to be a published author was what proved my achievement. My mother hadn't always been happy that I was a gay man, but it made things much better between us when she saw that I was making myself a storyteller out of the experience.

My mother was even more proud a decade later when I edited an anthology called *Hometowns: Gay Men Write about Where They Belong*. One of my own contributions to the anthology was an essay on Medfield, the common legacy that my mother and I shared. For once, she could find herself reflected in my stories.

My mother is the town clerk of Medfield, an elected post that makes her a visible community member. Proud of me and my accomplishments, she wanted everyone to know about my editing of this book and its essay about the town. So she bought an extra copy of *Hometowns* and donated it to the town library. There! she thought. Now anyone who went to the library would see this splendid book by her son. I imagine her sitting in her town hall office, smoking her unfiltered cigarettes and drinking her omnipresent cup of coffee, pleased as punch.

But a sudden cloud came over her thoughts. What if no one ever took the book out of the library? What if it sat in the stacks for years until someone came along and opened it to the back, where circulation history is recorded, and saw that the book had never once been borrowed? That would not do! So she sent her friends over to the library, one a day, to check out the book just so it could be stamped at the back. Only when she was sure there was enough evidence of the book's popularity could she relax again and go back to her cigarettes and coffee.

The Medfield town library is the first place I went as a young boy to look for stories about what it meant to be homosexual. There had been nothing on the shelves but those dry scientific texts that had left me so confused and alone. Now, thanks to my mother, when another young gay man or lesbian in Medfield goes on the same search for stories to help make sense of this life, there will be at the least one copy of *Hometowns*. That young man or woman will be able to read about someone who came before them, someone who lived in the same place, who went on to lead a decent life, and who even wrote a book about it all.

The young person who finds that book is going to feel the power of the story, the power that gives hope and destroys isolation.

1992

Medfield, Massachusetts

This essay about Medfield, Massachusetts, is the piece to which Preston refers at the end of "The Importance of Telling Our Stories." *Hometowns*, the book in which "Medfield" first appeared, was a Book of the Month Club selection and was probably Preston's proudest achievement.

Medfield is one of the ancient villages of New England. It was established as a European community in 1649, when pioneers from Dedham moved inland to the location near the headwaters of the Charles River, about twenty-five miles southwest of Boston.

The land on which Medfield was settled had been purchased from Chicatabot, the sachem of the Neponset Nation. He was one of those natives who saw the arrival of the English as, at worst, a neutral event. But it didn't take long for the indigenous people to see that the spread of the Puritan and Pilgrim colonies was threatening their very survival. In 1674, Metacom, the great leader known to the English as King Philip, organized an alliance of the native nations and led them to battle against the intruders.

The beginning of King Philip's War, as it was called, was fought in the Connecticut Valley. A few communities there were attacked and many of the settlers killed. Within a year

Metacom's warriors were pushing closer to Boston. Medfield was raided on February 19, 1675. Seventeen people were killed and half the buildings were destroyed.

Metacom was defeated later that winter in a climactic battle in nearby Rhode Island. His campaign was the last serious chance the natives had of sending the English away. Smallpox and other epidemics finished the destruction of the aboriginal nations over the next decades. Medfield's new proprietors, my ancestors, quietly prospered.

When the American Revolution broke out a century later, Medfield was firmly on the side of the rebels. The town meeting communicated regularly with the colonial legislature and the radical Committees of Correspondence, encouraging a strong stance against unfair taxation. When it was apparent that hostilities would break out, the citizens organized a contingent of minutemen who responded to the call to arms in Concord and Lexington (though they arrived too late to join in the battles).

The Revolution was the last striking event in Medfield's history. When independence was achieved, Medfield simply became the place it remained when I grew up there, a quintessential Yankee town, complete with a phalanx of the white clapboard churches everyone identifies with New England, all of it packaged in extravagant forest parks and with a wealth of substantial wood frame houses.

When I was born, in 1945, Medfield had fewer than three thousand inhabitants. It was assumed that all of us knew one another. It wasn't just that the population was small, it was also remarkably stable. Our families had all lived in the same place for so long that we all felt like an extended family. (And there were, in fact, many cousins in town. Not just first cousins, but second and third cousins. We all learned our interlocking heritage at an early age.) The names of all the participants in the colonial and revolutionary events were the same as many of those of my cousins and classmates and the people in the church my family attended—Harding, Morse, Adams, Lovell, Bullard, Wheelock, and Allen.

We lived our history. When the other kids and I played cowboys and Indians, we did it on the same battlegrounds where our ancestors had defeated King Philip. When we studied American history, our teachers taught us the names of the men from Medfield who had fought in the Revolution.

We weren't among those for whom this country's history is irrelevant. We weren't left out of the narrative of the white man's ascension. We were, in fact, those for whom American history was written. We were of British ancestry, if not English, then Scots or Irish. Our history textbooks were filled with names that sounded like our own. "Foreign" was, for us, someone of Italian descent. "Alien" was the Roman Catholic church.

As I grew older and came into contact with people from around the state, I discovered a different social criterion. People talked about ancestors who'd come from England on the *Mayflower*. I remember going to my mother and asking her if ours had. She looked at me strangely and replied, "Well, whenever any family's lived in a town like ours as long as we have, somebody married somebody who married somebody whose family came over on the *Mayflower*. But, why would you even care?"

Indeed. Why would anyone look for more? Wasn't coming from Medfield enough? There is a story about Yankee insularity that's told in many different forms. A reporter goes up to a lady who's sitting on a bench in a village common and asks her, "If you had the chance to travel to anywhere in the world, where would you go?" The lady looks around her hometown, mystified, and responds, "But why would I go anywhere? I'm already here!" The first few times I heard that story, I didn't understand it was a joke. I thought the woman was only speaking the obvious. It's the way we felt about Medfield.

Medfield was a very distinct reality to me. There was even a leftover colonial custom that gave the town a concrete definition. By 1692 the settlements around Boston were growing quickly and their perimeters were hazy because of conflicting land grants and native treaties. The executive power of each town was vested in the board of selectmen, three citizens elected by the town meeting to run things between that annual assembly of all the town's voters. The Great and General Court, the romantic name the Commonwealth of Massachusetts still uses for the state legislature, decreed that every five years the selectmen of each town would have to "perambulate the bounds" with the selectmen of its neighbors. The two sets of townspeople had to agree on the markers that separated them.

The requirement for the perambulation stayed on the books until 1973, and even then the rescinding law said, "However, it is enjoyable to keep the old tradition of meeting with the selectmen of adjoining towns for this purpose. It also affords an opportunity to agree to replacement of missing or broken bounds and to discuss subjects of mutual interest." (The Medfield Historical Commission recently reported, "It is also rumored that modern time selectmen partook of a drink or two at each boundary marker.")

When I was young, I used to walk the bounds of Medfield with the selectmen. The grown-ups' drinking habits weren't important to me, but I was in love with the stones we found with their antiquated signs and the aged oak and maple trees that appeared on the town records as markers between Medfield and Dover, Walpole, Norfolk, and other neighbors.

The living history of the monuments wasn't all I got from these walks. The perambulations gave firm evidence to just what was my hometown. I was also being told that everything on this side of the boundaries was Medfield. Everything on this side of the border was mine.

It's hard to overstate the sense of entitlement that a New

England boyhood gave me and my friends. I remember the first time I was taken to Boston. The city seemed large and frightening until my mother pointed to the large body of water between Boston and Cambridge and explained that it was the Charles, the same river that separated Medfield from Millis. I realized I couldn't be frightened of someplace that was built on the banks of *my* river.

Even if America wasn't all like Medfield, it certainly acted as though it wanted to be. The new suburban developments that were all the rage in the sixties mimicked the architecture of the buildings that had been standing around our village for centuries. Advertisements for the good life all seemed to take place in our town. Medfield had a wide flood plain to the west, hills to the south, forests to the north. It was the landscape surrounding the "nice people" we saw in magazines and on television. Our lawns were well kept and our trees carefully pruned. A snowstorm was a community event: my mother would make hot chocolate and fresh doughnuts (from scratch) for all the neighborhood children, and we'd build snowmen exactly like those pictured on the pages of the *Saturday Evening Post*.

Of course there were blemishes, some of them so well hidden that only those of us inside could see them. There were broken homes and drunken parents. There was economic upheaval as New England's industry migrated to the South after the Second World War. There were class divisions that were especially apparent to me, since my father's family—from Boston's industrial suburbs—was pure working class. We couldn't have been much better off than my aunts and uncles and cousins living in Boston's urban blight, but poverty wasn't as apparent when it was surrounded by beauty like Medfield's. Somerville didn't have Rocky Narrows State Park; Everett didn't have Rocky Woods State Reservation. And besides, not having a great deal of money had no impact on our status in town. My mother's social pedigree made my father's background irrelevant. Her children were of Medfield, and no one ever questioned that.

In fact, we were constantly reminded that our roots were right there on the banks of the Charles. My sisters and brothers and I were continually assaulted by older citizens who would stop us on the street and pinch our cheeks, "Oh, yes, I can see that you must be one of Raymond Blood's family. It's those eyes. Just like his!" My maternal grandfather had died fifteen years before I was born, but townspeople kept on seeing his lineage in my face. He'd been something of a hero in the town, a World War I veteran who'd prospected for gold in Nevada before he'd returned to take over the family's business, selling feed and grain to the small farmers in the region. To be Raymond Blood's grandson was no small matter. The pinches may have been annoying, but the rest of the message was clear: You are from this place.

Medfield was a town where a boy knew what it meant to belong. It was an environment out of which almost any achievement seemed possible. As we grew older, my friends and I picked and chose from the best colleges, dreamed the most extravagant futures, saw ourselves in any situation we could imagine. Our aspirations were the highest possible, and they didn't come out of pressure from striving families or a need to escape a stifling atmosphere. We envisioned ourselves however we chose because we felt it was ours, all of it, the entire American Dream. It was so much ours, we took it so much for granted, that we never questioned it.

There must have been many ways I was different from the other kids early on. I'm vaguely aware of being too smart, of not being physical enough, of hating sports. I got grief for all those things in the way any group of peers can deliver it, especially in adolescence. I certainly *felt* different. But the difference didn't define itself right away.

As we became teenagers, things happened that actually eased my sense of deviation. There were forces at work that made us more aware of the things that bound us together and made what might have separated us seem less important. Route 128 had been built in a long arc around Boston's suburbs in the fifties. Originally called a highway to nowhere, it was one of the first freeways whose purpose was to create a flow of traffic around centers of population, not between them. Route 128 quickly got another name: America's Highway of Technology. New companies with names like Raytheon and Northrop and Digital built enormous high-tech plants along the freeway's corridor. They moved the center of the region's economy out of Boston, toward places like Medfield. The town's population doubled, and then doubled again.

By the time we were in high school, we were faced with new classmates with strange accents and different standards. My friends had earned their extra spending money by trapping beavers and muskrats along the tributaries of the Charles and selling their pelts. The new kids didn't know about traps, and they didn't think it was important that their new homes in the spreading developments were ruining the animals' habitat. We were used to having fried clams as a special treat at the local drive-up restaurant; the new people were only angry that there weren't fast food chains. They had strange and exotic—and sexual—dances we hadn't heard of. We stood in the high school auditorium and wondered how they could act that way in public. When they hiked up on Noon Hill, they didn't know it had been the place from which King Philip had watched Medfield burn. They thought we were backward and quaint to care about such things.

The local kids closed ranks. I'm sure, as I look back now, that the newcomers must have been puzzled when Mike, the captain of every team sport possible, spent time with me, the class brain. They must have wondered just as much why I would pass afternoons with Philip, who didn't even go to Medfield High School but commuted to Norfolk County Agricultural School, the looked-down-upon "aggie" school in Walpole. And why would my (third) cousin Peter, probably the most handsome youth in town, walk home with me so often?

We defied the new standards; we held to our own. We had all been in the Cub Scout pack my mother had founded. We had all sat in the same kindergarten. We had all been a part of Medfield. I was one of the group and they wouldn't deny me.

When I return to my hometown now, I see that, in most ways, we won. People like Mike and Philip and Peter—and my mother and her friends—simply sat it all out. They waited for the newcomers to leave and then for a new wave to come in, the waves of migrating suburbanites who have changed addresses so often they can't tell the difference between Medfield and Northfield, Illinois, or Southfield, Michigan. My family and friends simply stayed; they had never intended to move. Now my mother is the town clerk, Mike runs the reunions of our high school class, and last I heard Philip took over his father's job as groundsman for the state hospital.

But I had begun to leave while I was still in high school. I had heard rumors about a different life and a different world. Its gateway, my books and magazines told me, was a bus station in the city. I began to travel to Boston more often, supposedly to visit my urban cousins, but I seldom got as far as their home in Somerville. I would stay, instead, in the Greyhound terminal and wait for one of a series of men to come and initiate me. They were traveling salesmen from Hartford, professors from MIT, students from Northeastern.

Eventually I'd travel farther to meet them. I took secret trips to New York when I was supposed to be skiing in New Hampshire. I hitchhiked to Provincetown, the fabulous center of the new world into which I was moving. And with every move, I left more of Medfield behind.

There was really no way I could see to combine my new life and my old. There was a man in Medfield who was whispered about, who belonged to our church and was the target for endless sympathy because he kept entering and leaving the state hospital. And there were two women down the street, nurses, who were so masculine that it was impossible to ignore their deviance from the town norms. But they offered me nothing. I wasn't like the nurses and I never, ever wanted to be like the man who was so continually institutionalized.

In some ways I moved into my new life with great joy. There was real excitement in it; certainly there was great passion. My explorations took me to places as far away as a New England boy could ever imagine. When it came to pick my college, I chose one in Illinois, the far horizon of my family's worldview, as far away as they could ever conceive of me going.

I also experienced rage over what was happening to me. I was being taken away from Medfield and everything it stood for. I was the one who should have gotten a law degree and come home to settle into comfortable Charles River Valley politics—perhaps with a seat in the Great and General Court? I should have lived in one of those honestly colonial houses on Pleasant Street. I should have walked through the meadows and the hills as long as I wanted, greeted by people I knew, all of us blanketed in our sense of continuity. History had belonged to us. But I was no longer one of them. I had become too different.

There had become a label for me that was even more powerful than the label of being from Medfield, something I don't think I could have ever envisioned being true.

I remember trying to find some way to come back to Medfield. I remember discovering a hairdresser in a Boston bar who had just opened a shop in town. I wanted desperately to fall in love with him and move back and find some way to be of Medfield again. Another time I did fall in love with a truck driver from Providence, a man of as much overstated masculinity as the nurses down the street. Maybe he and I could create a balance that the town would accept. He drank whiskey with my father, fixed cars with our neighbors, and knew all about the Red Sox. Maybe, between the two of us, we had enough that we could stay in Medfield. It didn't work. And in those days, no one ever thought it would work in any hometown.

I stopped trying to fit my life into Medfield. I turned my back on it. I belonged to a new world now, one that spun around New York, Chicago, San Francisco, Provincetown. I was danced and bedded away from home, into the arms of someplace no one had ever told me about.

1991

Portland, Maine: Life's Good Here

I have a young friend here in Portland who tells about riding his bicycle downtown on Saturday nights when he was sixteen and still in high school. He'd climb up on the roof of one of the warehouse buildings on Spring Street and sit and watch the men who walked in and out of the Underground, the big gay bar in town. He wanted to see what they were like, who they were, because he knew he was going to join them some day when he grew up and got the courage. It wasn't that they were all that exciting or different, it was just that they were who they were, and he knew he belonged with them.

What's striking about this story is that the young man knew where he was going and he knew where the points of entry were. Unlike earlier generations, the doorways for this young man were right here, in his hometown.

I never thought I'd live here. I didn't think gay men could live in such a small city, at least I thought they couldn't live a happy life. A small city like Portland would be for the closet.

I graduated from Medfield High School in 1963. It had always been assumed I would go to college. My parents' expectations of their own upward mobility counted on my generation's continued climb up the social ladder by getting at least an undergraduate degree. The only question was what school I'd go to. I chose one outside Chicago. Its proximity to a big city was probably the single most important criterion.

It wasn't that you couldn't get laid in rural Massachusetts back then; if all you wanted was homosexual sex, you were in pretty good shape in the sticks. I was one of an army of New

England boys who spent our spare time hitchhiking through the countryside. We weren't really going anywhere; sex was our destination. We were all just waiting for a driver who would pick us up and then be brave enough to let his hand fall on our thigh. I wanted more than that. I wanted to talk to the men with whom I had sex. I wanted to stop hiding. I knew I was gay and I knew that gay life was supposed to be an urban phenomenon. I didn't seen anything in Medfield that told me otherwise.

I went to Lake Forest, a socially elite but academically dysfunctional college in one of Chicago's northern suburbs. I found the bars in the city and began to set up the double life that was standard in the sixties: I was the sensitive, pleasant young man on campus who was socially (but never emotionally) available to women, but who blew open his closet door when he got downtown.

I soon learned there was another option. The same distance from Lake Forest as Chicago, in the other direction, was Kenosha, Wisconsin, a small industrial city where there were also gay bars. I had moved a thousand miles away from home to be close to the gay life of Chicago, but I found myself increasingly going out in Kenosha instead. I'd get to the freeway and assume I was going south to the big city, but I'd turn north, often amazing myself by the choice. The simple truth was that I was more comfortable with the blue-collar, small-city men in Wisconsin. The workers from the American Motors plant which dominated the Kenosha economy were much more familiar companions for me than the fake construction workers in Chicago who spent their time trading faux–Oscar Wilde witticisms with one another or who found opera the most compelling topic of conversation.

The men at American Motors were the kind of working-class men I had grown up with, the ones I always wanted to be close to. The Kenoshans and I talked the same talk, albeit with different accents. (And they were hot! It's especially noteworthy that in those pre-gym-culture days, they had hard-worked bodies that were significantly more interesting than the ones I found in Chicago's bars.)

After I graduated from Lake Forest I went on what I call the Grand Tour of the Gay Capitals. I began by moving to Boston. I was so tired of the rigors of sixties gay life—it was a lot of work to lie all the time—that I just wanted to find a lover and settle down. I found one, a man so handsome that more than twenty-five years later I can honestly say that he was one of the most gorgeous men I've ever been with. We were a stunning couple, both of us over six feet, both with long, rich hair. We were princes. We so impressed the then secret gay world we were entering that we were often taken on trips by older men. They just wanted to be near us, it seemed, perhaps to hear our delighted moans from behind our closed bedroom door.

But we weren't exempt from the tortures of that pre-activist life. My lover told me he had been waiting for someone to love because it would make all the rest of it okay. I was, he promised me, all he had wanted. But it turned out I wasn't enough to make up for the rest. He committed suicide after telling me that being queer was just too difficult. What is shocking today is that his death was *not* shocking at the time. The men who had taken us on trips weren't surprised at all. Suicide was a standard option for gay men in the sixties, even in a big city like Boston.

I just would not accept that. I was unwilling to accept suicide as a way out. I would have to find some people who would help me change the world, that was all there was to it.

My next stop was Minneapolis. It was 1969 and the University of Minnesota was a national hotbed of homosexual rights activism, even before the Stonewall Riots of that year, usually thought of as the beginning of the modern gay movement. I wanted to take the enthusiastic vision of the just-being-born movement on campus and move it into the neighborhoods.

We had an assumption at Gay House, the community center we founded. We knew that people from all over the Midwest were coming to Minneapolis to come out. But we didn't think Gay House or the city itself was their goal; we saw ourselves as inhabiting a way station on an underground railroad that would take them still farther out. At Gay House they could learn about gay life and read new gay books and spend time in a discussion group, but we assumed most of them would move on. Minneapolis was too small for gay life, we thought, even though it was a booming city in the seventies, a city to which straights were anxious to move. We thought gay men had to go to places like San Francisco, where we heard there were now bars that had open windows onto the street, or New York where there were so many activist gay men after the Stonewall Riots that they could even imagine becoming a political force. We were just one step on a pyramid that pointed up, to liberation, to metropolis.

I took up that tour again myself—Philadelphia, New York, Los Angeles, and San Francisco and the exploding sex and political scene on Castro Street. Then back to New York. I lived in each of these cities for at least a year. I didn't put down any roots. Having a hometown wasn't the point. Being gay was our geographic location. There were many shorter stops along the way—Key West (where it sometimes seemed everyone was gay), Houston (for Splash Day, the first time I saw two men dance close together with their shirts off—and they were only wearing bathing suits! And you could see their erections right through their bikinis!), Provincetown (which had a strangely compelling attraction for me—all those familiar accents, the crazy ways the streets were laid out, New England).

But in 1979 I discovered I was tired of it all. I had gotten from the emerging gay ghettos of America what I had needed. I had gone through the academy. Hell, I had a graduate degree complete with a leather tassel on my cap and a pink triangle tattooed on my chest to prove it. I had experienced it; I had seen it; I had done it; I want to go . . . where?

I began to think more about my time in Minneapolis. I realized we had been wrong in our assumptions about the people who moved there. Many had stayed. We had changed the city so much that they hadn't felt the need to move on to the coasts as I had. Was that kind of smaller-city life an option for me? Had we advanced the movement enough that gay life didn't *have* to be lived in the big cities? I wanted a quieter place to pursue my writing, and a less expensive one. I wanted to live in a place like Kenosha, where I understood how people thought, *and* I wanted one like Provincetown, where I understood their accents.

Portland, Maine, fit all my criteria. There was the beginning of a gay community; it had direct flights to New York and was only a two-hour drive to Boston, just in case I needed to escape; it was beautiful. It was in New England, where I had grown up.

Portland is a city of only 60,000 (200,000 if you call it a metropolitan area and define the population in that way). I always call it the toy city, because it's so small, but it *is* a city. It has all the urban accoutrements that keep it from being just a place where a lot of people happen to live—someplace like Manchester, New Hampshire, for example, which has more population but none of the cultured air of Portland. Portland has museums, colleges, a symphony, a downtown, and history. God, does it have history. Everywhere you turn another plaque announces a landmarked building or someone's birthplace, and statues all over the place remind you of the political and literary figures from the city. Longfellow is very big in Portland.

. . .

There were problems as soon as I got here. I stayed in a motel for the first month I lived in Portland to get the lay of the land while I figured out what neighborhood I wanted to live in, if I wanted to stay here. I remember sprawling on the motel bed and watching a television news report about gay life in Maine. The very existence of the broadcast was a good sign, until the camera showed the only gay man who was willing to come out for the report—and he would do it only if his face was hidden in silhouette. This wasn't the kind of gay politics I had been used to; this wasn't the way I expected the world to have changed.

For a short time I was depressed by that television program. It was an argument that this wasn't a place where I could live. Then I realized there was no reason for me to hide myself. I could become a face of gay life in this state as easily as I had in Minnesota and the other places I had lived. We all have that option of reinventing ourselves and altering the landscape we inhabit.

I discovered something about that landscape as it existed, something I've come to realize is vitally important to how this place works. I had chosen Portland because it was the smallest city I could imagine living in. But everyone else I met was here because this was the biggest city they ever intended to put up with. Far from being a step on the pyramid I had envisioned in my Minnesota days, a pyramid leading to metropolis, Portland *was* the metropolis so far as most people here were concerned. My modern gay belief in the big-city-as-Jerusalem wasn't shared by my new peers. The idea that this was *it*, this was where we were all going to end up, bolstered my vision. Okay, then, we damned well better make it the best place we could. My new friends agreed.

I began to write for a new local weekly paper, the *Chronicle*. The pay was wretched, but they needed writers badly and were glad to have me. Max Hartshorne, the editor, accepted almost anything I could get to him on deadline, even if that meant publishing yet another review of a new gay novel. ("Not *too* often, Preston. Please!" he used to say, but he ran them.)

All journalists are media junkies; it's part of the job description. The writers for the daily newspapers and the bigger statewide weekly newspapers read the *Chronicle* every issue and got to know my byline, and my willingness to write about being gay. I began to show up on the television screen now, and not in silhouette. Soon there were other gay men and lesbians willing to be interviewed. We began to give Portland and its lesbian and gay life a human face.

There were repercussions from all that public notice. I had a real shock when a few gay men who had recently propositioned me in the bars in Portland began to ask me not to speak to them on the street. They didn't want my notoriety rubbing off on them. This was another point at which I thought I'd have to leave. To turn away from another gay man, to leave me isolated on the streets of Portland, was a violation of the most essential tenets of the new gay life—that we had to stand together, we had to protect the most vulnerable. I was crushed.

The men who rejected me were all of a certain kind, I realized. They all considered themselves artistic, and they thought Portland was really too provincial. In a way, they had no involvement in the gay life of the city because they felt it would challenge what they thought was their social standing. These were men who could afford to fly off to Fire Island when they felt the urge, or to New Orleans for Mardis Gras when they wanted to party. Being gay was a vacation for them, not a life.

Other men felt differently. L. L. Bean is one of the largest employers in the state, and of course many lesbians and gay men work there. When I moved to Portland I arrived with a single suitcase; it contained all the clothes I needed, mainly black turtlenecks and jeans. But after I began to pose as a spokesman for gay Portland, the guys at Bean's decided I needed to look the part. There's something called the Company Store in Freeport where, for ridiculously cheap prices, employees are able to buy all the returned merchandise the store so publicly accepts, no questions asked. My new friends took down my clothing sizes and went to the Company Store, where they slowly began to accumulate a respectable wardrobe for me—oxford-cloth shirts and chinos, loafers and rep ties. By god, if I was going to do this public thing, they wanted me to look right! These were the men who cared about the world gay activists were building; they were the ones who expected to benefit from our work. They were the ones who knew they had nothing to gain from hiding.

Something else happened about the same time. There is a large, state-of-the-art photocopying shop here in Portland. In 1981 it was the only place in the city whose equipment was sophisticated enough to reproduce manuscripts efficiently. One day when I was there having some things duplicated, the manager came up to me and told me my business was no longer welcome. "I don't know if what you're doing is illegal, but I hope it is," she announced. (I *was* writing erotica, but it so happened the letter in the machine just then was to Gerard Conley, then president of the Maine Senate, thanking him for sponsoring a gay civil rights bill.)

This was censorship in the most base form; this was a threat to my livelihood. I stormed out and I walked down Congress Street, the main boulevard that runs the length of the downtown peninsula. I went into the next printing shop I found. I saw a manual photocopying machine. I demanded to talk to the manager. Barely containing myself, I told her what had just happened. "Will you let me use that machine?" "Hell, I'll do it for you," she responded. "I don't give a damn what you write."

The photocopying incident told me it was possible for me to live in Maine. It wasn't just that there was a good, old-fashioned libertarian who owned a Xerox machine and would let me use it. I soon learned something else about the first copy shop. People began to come up to me in bars and on the streets and tell me they had read an article or a story that I had written. I would be puzzled because what they were referring to hadn't yet been published. I finally learned that the many gay employees of the fancy photocopier had been making multiple copies of my work for themselves and their friends. Those pieces that had so offended the manager were circulating promiscuously through the city, and she was paying for it. No matter how hurt and angry I was with the "sophisticated" members of the Portland art scene, I now discovered that I had an appreciative audience in my new hometown.

That was the year that the old *Evening Express* felt confident enough to headline an article: "Portland Is the Gay Mecca North of Boston." Well, yeah, but that wasn't saying very much in 1981. What were they comparing it to, Nashua?

"Are you ready to come back yet?" That was the question I was always asked by my big city friends. They were convinced that I, the quintessential modern urban fag, would be unable to live in Portland. I would have to have leather bars, I would have to go to the theater, I would have to take part in the excitement of national politics. I certainly had to live in the big city to have sex.

They couldn't understand how I could be happy in Maine. But, of course, they had never met the men here. My friends in New York were sure that one had be able to carry off the costumes of the new gay life to be attractive. They had never seen my friend Brian who worked on the fishing piers here and who would come by my apartment after work wearing three layers of torn up thermal underwear underneath his yellow slicker. I kept telling Brian that if he packaged the concept and sold it on Christopher Street, he'd make a fortune. And there was Mike, who worked construction for Central Maine Power. When he realized how much I enjoyed his work clothes, he gave me his hard hat, something I could only have gotten in Manhattan from a boutique.

And there were the sound of the men! I had lost my accent when I went to Lake Forest, humiliated into practicing a public television kind of spoken English in my room by the snotty kids I went to college with. Now I could hear the sounds of New England straight from the lips of the men I met, the same men who would kiss me. I used to seduce men into my bed and then, to their confusion, just ask them to speak, to let me hear their Maine accents. That was sex enough for me, at least for a while.

"No, I don't think I'll leave," I told my friends. "I think I'm going to stay."

The Matlovitch Society was formed in Portland a few years ago, named after Leonard Matlovitch, an air force sergeant who fought his discharge for being gay in the mid-1970s. The group intended to create a lecture series of gay and lesbian speakers, with the hope that, in the fine tradition of New England athenaeums, the shared information would create a bond within the gay and lesbian community and would uplift it.

"We want a hundred people to show up every other week," the organizers told me.

Sure, I responded. You couldn't get that many fags and dykes to show up for a lecture in New York. This is Portland. Get real. Today they regularly draw two hundred people at their events.

These are people who take their lives seriously, who want to learn about their history and want to change the world they live in. Just being together and not hiding—they most often meet in the auditorium of the Portland Public Library—allows them to create a vision for their life in this small city. It was Matlovitch Society members who first asked why there wasn't a gay civil rights bill in Portland. A municipal ordinance had not been proposed primarily because the major gay rights organizations were focused on a statewide bill. But so many people came to Matlovitch meetings, certainly the liberal city council could be approached by some of them. The bill was passed. It immediately provoked a referendum initiated by the religious right, but after a grueling election campaign, the voters of the city upheld the ordinance.

The Matlovitch Society has some other goals—a community center is one of the big ones. Someone just started up yet another attempt at a Portland gay/lesbian newspaper. We even have a gay pride parade, albeit small—this is Maine, after all. It's not that we're concerned about being out, we just don't like those public displays of emotion.

A young man came to me and said he was terribly concerned about something I had to help him with. He was guilty of internalized homophobia, he explained. He was a waiter in a local restaurant and was annoyed by gay and lesbian couples who would come in and kiss and hold hands and all of that.

I thought for a minute and asked him how he felt when a straight couple did the same thing—kissed at their table, carried on, all of it. "Oh, I *hate* it," he answered.

Well, I explained, it's not homophobic if you're applying the same standards to everyone. Let's face it, this is Maine, we're restrained people. We can get it up for civil rights when we need to, but really, we just want to be left alone to lead our private lives as we think they should be. We're just not into all the demonstrative stuff.

"Besides," I said, "they were probably all just tourists—straight or gay. None of them know how to act anyway."

That was something he could agree with.

"Are you finally going to come back?" my New York friends still ask.

"No. Life's good here," I answer.

1993

THE MEN OF MAINE

When Preston moved to Portland, the men of Maine immediately asserted themselves as his audience. He knew right away that he wanted to communicate with the "gay guy on the street"—or, more aptly, the gay guy in the mill and on the docks—and tell their stories.

"And they had such stories to tell!" he once wrote. "We in the big cities had thought that all of gay life revolved around the institutions that we were developing as part of our new ghettos. The same impulses to create a new society were happening in Maine, but they were often different, stories of struggle that weren't recognized in other parts of the country. I quickly realized that it was my role to be the scribe for the gay people in this isolated state."

Preston took his scribal charge literally. He began an ambitious oral history project, interviewing gay men from various parts of the state. He planned to transcribe the interviews and compile them in a book called "The Men of Maine: Gay Life Far from the Fast Track." He was awarded a grant from the Maine Arts Commission to support the project, which eventually was expanded to include the life histories of Maine residents with AIDS.

"The Men of Maine" was never finished, but Preston did have some of the tapes transcribed. The following interview with Bob Gravel, a lifelong resident of Lewiston, Maine, is a riveting account of one man's struggle to live in a homophobic small town. The harrowing events Gravel describes are rendered all the more tragic by the way he finally decides to cope with the situation. It was Preston's desire to prevent precisely this kind of tragedy that drove his fierce activism.

An Interview with Bob Gravel

Tell me about growing up in Lewiston. What's your family like?

Well, my family is old, old-school French Catholic. You live a certain way and that's it. That's how I grew up: You go to school, come home, nothing much more when I was younger. We lived out in what they called the country. There were a few houses around, but really not much else.

Describe Lewiston. People who read this aren't going to know anything about it.

Well, it's a mill town, really boring. It was home. It was all I knew. To me it was the world. I knew nothing else. Matter of fact, I'd never been out of Maine, until two years ago when the owners of the bar hired a bus. We were going to go to a Red Sox game in Boston. But we started barhopping—and forget the game!

That was the first time you'd been out of state?

The first time, the only time. I thought Lewiston was the whole thing. We have relatives in Portland, and we'd go up that way and then come home. That was big times for us, that and going to the beach.

Don't I remember that you're from a very large family?

We're twelve, all married but me, some more than once. I'm the baby of the boys. I have two younger sisters.

How French was your family? Did you grow up speaking French?

Yeah, a lot of the time. When I was younger, it was mostly French we spoke. As the years went on, the younger kids started going to public schools, the older ones went to Catholic [French-speaking] schools.

Did you have trouble going to an English-speaking public school?

No. Of course there were little things left over from French; we'd say towel paper instead of paper towel, things like that were problems at first.

There was no problem growing up French in Lewiston because most of the people were French. Matter of fact, when you had people who weren't, we'd just kinda said, "Oh, those English people!"

Lewiston was mostly French to begin with. Because the people in Canada came to town because of the mills and the river. They needed a river to generate electricity for the mills, you see. Once you got a lot of French people, most of them stayed together.

Was your family rich? Poor? Middle class?

My father had two jobs. Us kids used to go out selling eggs, tomatoes, we had a couple gardens. Not big gardens, but enough to take care of our needs and sell a little on the side. We didn't have to go out and steal. If we wanted pocket money, there was no problem. We got it. But we were all kids that worked. They didn't have to fight with us about the trash or doing the dishes. We worked. We knew it had to be done and we did.

When did you move out of your family?

Just last year. My mother was living with me, and she was just getting along in years. I couldn't bring any friends over. It was very hard. But finally I told my sister and she said she'd take care of her for a little while. She did, so then I lived alone and I loved it.

You were working in a shoe mill?

Yeah, a shoe factory. I started there when I was thirteen years old. I worked there until I was thirty. Then I got offered a better job, but that guy had a heart attack, so I went right back to another place and went to work for minimum wage. After making five something an hour, to go back to minimum wage . . . I wasn't crazy about it, but what are you going to do? Then a job offer came from the first place, so I went back.

Did you finish high school?

No. I had to go to work to help support the family. My father and my mother had split up. My older brothers and sisters went out working. We needed money at home to help the younger ones and back then we didn't have state money like they do today, so we all had to help. What I did, I went to high school, then I worked two jobs. Then I joined the police reserve. I was ready to go to college. Then, it was too much for me. I quit the night job. I couldn't complete high school at night, but I completed the GED [general equivalency diploma], I accomplished that.

When did you start to think that you might be gay?

I guess I was about sixteen. I just had different feelings, but I never showed them. As a matter of fact, I used to show guys girlie books and get a hard-on with them, that type of thing. But it was really not in me. I just was never really very interested in girls. On occasion, I went parking and stuff, double-dating back in high school, but, I don't know. It wasn't really what I wanted. I didn't understand because it was wrong to do anything else and I was different. I didn't have my first real sexual encounter till I was twenty-one.

Really? Hadn't you done anything?

I had jerked off with guys, you know, that stuff when I was a kid. But I'm talking about a real relationship which wasn't until I was twenty-one. It was with my barber.

It was raining out once and he gave me a ride and first thing I knew this hand was on my leg and I liked it and that was it.

Did you have any trouble with it?

It was fun that night; of course it was my first time. After the orgasm, though, I went home and got into a tub of hot water and felt real bad. I went to confession, went to church, you name it. I had real guilt. Then, maybe two, three months later, it happened again with the barber.

I saw him before, but I'd always get away because I felt strange at what had happened. I didn't go back for a haircut either. But, like I said, it was a few months later and it happened again. I started getting my haircuts again. I liked it. Then, from there I learned where to meet people—in the park.

How'd you learn that?

From the barber. He told me where guys hang out. I went. I'd see some guys in the park waiting for some other guy and they'd take off. It was really in a church parking lot, next to the park. So I observed this.

Then I said, "To hell with this, I'll get my own car." I even worked two jobs for it. I worked at the shoe factory in the day and at night I'd work for the hospital. I made some extra money, I saved, I bought a car. It was worth it too.

I met a few that weren't too bad back then. There weren't a lot of hustlers around. It was mostly people who were fun. I meet a few guilt queens who'd kick you out of their car after they had their orgasm, but I ran into very few of them.

Did you ever fall in love with any of these guys?

No. I was just having a good time. Then, I guess I was twenty-eight, twenty-nine, when that happened with a neighbor kid.

My parents had moved downtown when I was thirteen or something then. There were these cute little neighbor kids who were two and three years old. As I was getting older, they were getting older. When I was twenty-eight or twenty-nine, they were sixteen, seventeen, whatever. The name-calling started. Faggot. Queer. Because I was always alone, never with girls, they suspected right away. People are like that around here. If you're not married by a certain age, there's something wrong with you. So talk had started. But no one actually knew.

But I never denied it, I'm not a good liar.

Anyway, one of those little boys grew up to be a football player in high school. He kept calling me names and throwing rocks. I caught him one night when he was joyriding in his parents' car by the park. I pulled over and he came by and showed me that he had a baseball bat in the car. Didn't worry me, I just watched him go by.

Then, the next time he came by he was with a female and he was less violent. That was all right. I made a little signal, letting him know I was interested.

Another time, he pulled over and I said, "Hey, you want to try it? I'll show you what it's like?" And we became pretty good friends for a long time, up until just six months ago. We were . . . of course, he's a straight dude. But he was the only person I fell in love with.

He was a rugged kid. He'd come over at one or two in the morning, after he'd left his friends. It went on like that for I don't know how long, six years? It just ended a few months ago.

Did you like that relationship?

Oh, yeah. Matter of fact, when I left Lewiston, I really wanted him to come with me. He's a good person, but he has to keep that straight image. People suspected him because they'd see him around the house. He had friends that lived down the street from me. They'd kid him, "Oh, you went to see Gravel, huh?" Stuff like that. And really, it was true, so it really bothered him a lot. He said, "No more. I don't want to see you no more."

When did you move from going to the park into going to bars and those kinds of things?

Well, I never had any gay friends, never. Until the bar opened in Lewiston about ten years ago. It was called the Blue Swan at that time. I was scared to go in so I brought a couple tough guys from work with me. Everybody at work knew I was gay. As time went on people would ask me. I didn't go around with a sign on my chest saying I was gay, but when people would ask, I'd say, "Yeah, I go with men." I never had any trouble at work. A very few guys would call me names, but nothing vicious. Anyway, I brought some real tough guys from work with me. I was scared. You heard stories about those kind of people who tie you up and tear your clothes up. I didn't know what went on in that bar. That's why I got a couple friends to go with me.

I went in and I met people who said hello and all of this and I looked around and sat down and had a beer with my friends and it wasn't that bad. There was nothing going on. You didn't see guys making out or tearing clothes off each other. So then I started going alone. I brought another friend of mine who I found out was bi[sexual]; we started going pretty regular after that. But I never took anyone home from the bar, never.

You still haven't?

No. Never. It's been over ten years.

But you still go there?

I think I might have met one guy who was checking the place out, one of those curious people. That was it, though.

One guy. He wasn't a regular. He was just someone who had dropped in.

What difference in your life did it make to have the bar to go to?

I made friends through the years. It was a place to be around the same kind, people who have the same interests. We had some people there that were a little more bizarre. But it was a place to go and not feel like you were being watched or suspected or anything. Like, when you go in a straight bar and you buy someone a beer and they know you're gay, well . . . I did go to straight bars too. In town—in Lewiston—everybody knew I was gay and any bar I went to or store I went to, people knew. Just through the years.

Wasn't that terribly uncomfortable?

At first, I was always afraid to get beat up. But I found by being honest I had no problems, except for the last couple years. . . .

I had quite a sex life though. The last six years it was basically that football player and, as a matter of fact, another friend of his that used to throw rocks at me. But with him, it was just once every three or four months. But this football player was every weekend by then.

Why do you think you go for these guys instead of the people you might meet in the bar? What's the attraction?

I don't know. . . . Bar people, or gays in the bar are . . . I've met a lot of them that aren't really men at all. They aren't honest. There are some though. But there are some who are just out to get what they can. I think a lot of the gays today go for somebody who's pretty, handsome, well built. I mean, let's face it, I'm not going to get a ride home from them. I think basically that's what it is. People really don't come on to me because I'm not good looking.

But what about the other men? Why would you have better luck with them?

Because this is an opportunity for them. They know what I am so it's not like going up to another guy on the street and saying, "Hey, do you want to get it on?" There's a chance of getting punched, or someone telling someone else or whatever. They know I'm quiet about it. They trust me. I think that's probably the reason why I have these guys.

That's a benefit to having all those people know you're gay?

Yeah. I mean, all those phone calls I used to get! Heavy breathing . . . but the bar gays, they look for someone with a nice body and they look for youth. When you get older, it's pretty sad.

Oh, come on, I'm older than you are, and I'm not unhappy the way you're talking about it. You can't say that age is everything.

Listen! I'm going to work on that. [Pats his belly.] But if I was in better shape and all that I think I'd have a lot more dates. I think people are attracted to the cuteness rather than what's inside you. Just like a good-looking guy and some straight girl. She's probably the smarkiest person, she'd make the worst wife and mother, yet some girl who looks regular, she'd be the best mother and best everything. The guy goes for the one with the cute ass. I think it goes on in gay life like that a lot.

Are you saying you were happy enough with the men you were seeing on the side that you didn't have to put up with the bar games?

I liked to go to the bar and just talk. I wasn't totally happy. I was content with what was going on. I guess the football player had a lot to do with that.

So you did want to fall in love.

I was in love with that man.

You felt bad when it ended?

I did my crying.

He was . . . He would have been a good gay guy. But he couldn't handle it. He had the same upbringing as me: French Catholic family, macho brother. I think his sister would have understood, but his father was a real redneck and his brother too. So there was no way. Can you imagine him going to his brother and saying, "I'm gay." His brother would beat the hell out of him.

What about your own brothers?

When they first found out I was gay, they were going to hire a prostitute. Really! I must have been twenty-two, close to it, when I started saying, "Hey, I don't go out with girls and that's it." They wanted to get some prostitute at some American Legion club. I said, "No way! You do that and I'll have her arrested for molesting me!"

Did they get angry?

Oh, yeah. They didn't think it was normal. Even today there's two of them that are ashamed of me. But, yet, it's my life, you know? I don't think they have the right to criticize me. Plus my older brother's son is gay; he's about twenty-five, twenty-six. My brother is totally against it. That's why my nephew left the state. His mother goes to visit but his father never will.

Did your nephew ever come and talk to you?

Never. They always kept him away from me. My mother asked me one time, "Did you make him that way?" But I never saw him that much when we were younger; I was never really involved in talking to him.

What do you feel about that? Do you think you might have given him anything if you could have talked? That you could have helped him?

I really feel bad for him because of his father, my brother. My nephew could never talk to his father. I felt bad, but I figure he has his own life, he's old enough, he's got a good job. He doesn't need his father. He doesn't need him. His mother does need him though. My sister-in-law is a good person.

Would you have talked to him if he would have come to you?

Oh, yes.

I'm surprised he didn't.

Can you imagine going up to your uncle and saying you're gay, when your uncle's brother is against it? I think he felt that I might have preached at him or something like his father did. I wouldn't have, but he doesn't know this.

The rest of my family . . . I have another brother who is very sympathetic, very helpful. He'd give you the shirt off his back, really a good man. All my sisters are all right now.

One, well, she used to work in this bar. A lot of people there would call me fag and queer. She came up to me one day and said, "I'm so ashamed of you." And I said, "How can you be ashamed of me when you've been going out with a married man for eight years! Who are you to talk to me?"

She said, "How do you know about that?"

I said, "The whole town knows about it!"

She thought it was a big secret; she had put curtains in the garage so if his car was parked there nobody could see it. But everybody knew. But, really, she was the only one I had a little bit of trouble with, and I made her understand that my life was mine.

Most of the guys I had trouble with were high school kids, and some a little older, ones unsure of their own sexuality. My football player is a good example. He was really quiet for over a year. Finally we started talking, I gave him a few drinks, loosened him up. I asked him, "Why do you throw rocks at me and call me names, when all the time you're coming over here?"

He said, "Well, it's so my friends never suspect me."

The thing is, a couple of his friends were also going out with me secretly once in a while. I never told on them though. That's something I never did. But I'd say, "Well, you're not the only one. Some of your friends do this too." But I never named names, not even to him. It was really strange that they were calling me names when they were together, but they're knocking at my door when they're alone.

You said things started to get worse a while ago.

Two years.

What changed?

I think people are more violent. I don't know if it's from watching TV or the drugs or ... I have no idea. But the younger people are more aggressive today, really. More violent. These guys were high school guys who knew there was a fag over here. They started to follow the car, and threw big rocks, not little rocks either, big rocks. Smashed my windows, chased me. . . .

But you've said you were used to that.

I got the name-calling. Pebbles were thrown at me. But this here was really much more violent.

How did you respond to it?

Well, of course, I ran off. I'd go up one-way streets to get rid of them. I'd go to the police.

They said, "Stay home, if you wouldn't go out it wouldn't happen."

I thought, "Hey, this is a free country." Finally I had to go bring them to court. And I'd fight them.

There was a pizza place. I've been going there for ten years. There was a bunch of guys outside and they said, "You come in here faggot, you're dead." Nobody's going to tell me where I can go and where I can't go. I got out of my car and they surrounded me. They had sticks and then the police came. Some guy I never knew had come to my assistance, so they backed off. But it was all part of the same group of people who all went to high school together. It was their Saturday night: "We'll go chase Bob around. Go bother the gay people." It was something to do.

What happened when you took them to court?

This one guy had been driving with a suspended license. He had five other counts against him. I finally faced him in court. I was ready to have him prosecuted. Then they got to wheeling and dealing and the assistant DA came up to me and she said, "If you drop your charge, then he's going to plead guilty to the others."

So I said, "Okay, I'll drop the charge. But you tell him to stay away from me for the rest of his days." After that, I'd see him on the street and he wouldn't say nothing. But I faced him up to the last moment.

What had he done that you took him to court?

What had he done?! My God! Chased me, said he was going to kill me, tried to run me over in his car. Harassment, there was a lot of it. He'd wait for me next to my house with two carloads of people! When I'd begin to come through, rocks would hit me in the legs, hit me in the back. It was unreal. But they were violent—more than I had ever gone through, but not as violent as the last ones were.

These last guys . . . they had a lot of aggression, a lot of anger. Most of these kids came from broken homes, or a home where the parents drank a lot. There was one kid with them who had his parents and I called up his mother and she said, "If my son was in front of me right now, I'd punch him in the face for what he's done to you."

Did you contact other parents?

Oh, yeah! I really succeeded much better when I talked to the parents. After they got to know me over the phone, there was not one parent who said anything nasty to me. They were all concerned about what their kids were doing—I'm talking about the kids who had two parents, fairly decent homes—no problem there. But the ones who had just a mother and a grandmother . . . those are the kids I had a lot of trouble with.

This violence was persistent over a two-year period?

It was all the time. I was in a store one time, some guys came in and threw cans at me and rolled them at my feet on the floor. . . .
I took that group to court and it stopped.

But you didn't leave Lewiston then?

Of course not. I always lived there. I had a fairly good job. I was making six bucks an hour. Not the best, but it wasn't too bad. I had a nice apartment.
Well! I had a right to be what I wanted to be. I didn't bother anyone. I didn't go around really harassing people—you know, whistling, saying, "Hey, want to come for a ride? Want to get it on?" If I did that, I deserve a punch in the nose.
Oh, I did do that a couple times. But it was nothing! I got feeling good and I saw something nice and said, "Hey, how are you, honey?" But it was nothing! Some guys walk off, some guys said, "Ya faggot!" But it happened just a couple times over

the years. It wasn't an everyday thing I did. Basically, they'd come to me for sex. I didn't . . .

But I still felt, I got a right to go to the store. If I can't go where I want to go without all these threats, I might as well not be living. I felt that strongly about it. If you can't have your freedom, then you might as well be dead. If I got beaten to death, well, at least I'd be better off. I mean, you're not going to tell me I can't go into that store. I think taking them to court showed them that I wasn't a sissy.

What other escalation started then?

One guy lived two buildings away from me. He never said nothing until one day, when a punk was with him, and the punk said, "Oh, there's that faggot."

And that was it!

That started it all over again. It was because someone pointed me out to my neighbor, started the name-calling, started chasing me. I was going up one-way streets again, getting away, going to the police. It was difficult because this here was a neighbor.

It got worse. I left a note on his car. I said, "Please, we live in the same neighborhood, just cut it out. Leave me alone. I don't bother you. You live your life, I live mine."

I think he wanted my attention. He was always grabbing his front and saying to me, "Hey, Gravel, you want this don't you?" and, "Screw you, Gravel." I never paid attention.

Then, one day, I said, "Why don't you grow up?"

That did it. He came after me.

The other two that were with him stopped at the edge of my driveway, but this one came right up and started poking at me, and he said that I'd thrown eggs at his truck and I was bugging him and I left that note on his truck and it was a nasty note.

I tried to walk away. I had just cashed my check and bought groceries. I had $160 in my pocket. That's a lot of money for me. I wasn't going to let him have my groceries either 'cause I had a maple walnut cake and I love maple walnut cake. I said, "Stay right there." I walked away and I went across the lawn to a neighbor and asked her to call the police, but she didn't want to get involved.

I went back to my house. He jumped me from behind, kicked me in the back. I fell on the stairs and hit the back of my head. He jumped on me. But he never punched me. He just laid on top of me. I didn't understand that.

He didn't hurt me too bad, but he got me pissed. I let the groceries go and I was going to turn around and let him have it. I mean, I got a good-sized fist. I'm not a violent man, but I'd had enough. I started hollering, really hollering, the whole neighborhood heard me. The cops came and he ran off. But before he did, he said, "I'm going to kill you. I don't care how long it takes."

I believed him. I . . . some people say those things sometimes, but it was the way he said it. I sensed it. I just sensed that. I'm going to kill you! He meant it.

What happened next?

He went around bragging that he had beat up a fag. I found out his name. I went to the police again. They couldn't find him. I said, "Fuck this, I'm going to go see a lawyer." I went and got a paper served on him. When he got the paper, he called the lawyer up and said, "I don't know who this guy Gravel is, but whoever he is, I'll really give him trouble. If I'm going to get blamed for something, I'll do something." Of course, it was just a coverup, this was the right guy. He'd done those things.

Then he came after me some more, name-calling, coming around the house and hiding, breaking things around the house. I'd come home and I'd sense that he was there. I'd just have this eerie feeling. I was right most of the time. I'd hurry up, put the car in the garage, and run upstairs. That's how I lived for a while.

One night, I went to the bar. It was a Friday night, November first. They chased me when I got out of the bar; they were waiting for me in the parking lot. I got to the car and went up a one-way street, they tried to cut me off. We were facing each other, we almost hit head on. I went home, got the gun.

I had gotten a gun the day he said he was going to kill me back in August. I had it unloaded. But this particular night, I went home and got the gun, put in bullets, went back to the bar. I took my friend home. That meant I had to go home alone afterward.

They were waiting for me. They threw rocks, mud piles. I got to a police station and they drove me home. I went upstairs and that was it.

Then, Saturday night, I called the parents to let them know what was going on. His grandmother said, "He has the right to be mad at you, you left a note on his truck."

I said, "They've been bugging me for a long time. I want him to stop. That's why I left a note. If I'm going to do something, I'm going to do it big."

I stayed at home. I didn't go out. I sensed something. Here we go again. Besides, I was tired. I'd cleaned my house and washed the windows, so I was pretty tired. I could have gone out, but I didn't need the hassles. I turned out all the lights and I was watching television. I had the contrast on low, dark, and I saw the car come by. Six, seven times it stopped in front of the house and then left.

Then Sunday, same thing. My sister came over with her boyfriend in the afternoon and we had a few drinks. I gave them a ride home. I didn't want to go out, but I said I'd give them a ride home. I came back, parked my car in the garage, locked it, and went upstairs. Then I had something to eat and I took a bath and was getting into bed. I was just lying there, reading a magazine, and listening to the radio. I heard a little tap at the door.

I got up and said, "Who's there?" There was no answer. I opened the door, turned the light on, there was nobody in the hall. I just closed the door. I looked outside and I saw someone coming in the building, I saw several people, but I saw that one in particular go up toward the stairs.

I ran to the phone and called the police. I said, "These people are here, in the hall."

They said, "We're busy right now."

I said, "Hey, I don't care. I've got a gun. I'm tired of these people. I'm going to go down and confront them."

But it was too late.

Then there was a regular knock on the door. I said, "Who's there?"

The guy said, "My name is Mike." Feminine like, trying to imitate a faggot.

I said, "Mike? Mike who? What do you want? I don't know you."

Another one said, "You know me, I'm George."

"I don't know you."

He said, "Are you Bob?"

I said, "Bob doesn't live here any more."

They said, "Oh, darn it, we were told to come here for a good time."

I said, "Who told you that?"

"Someone from the bar."

I thought, Oh, God, it's them. I just hope they leave. I just sensed it was them. I said, "That's malarkey, you're not going to find a good time here." It sounded like they were leaving, I heard footsteps. I went to the living room and looked out the window, I could see the porch from there. They never came down.

Then they started kicking at the door. Kicking and kicking

and kicking . . . it was unreal. At this point I grabbed my gun and I grabbed the phone again and I called the police. I said, "My God, they're kicking in my door! What do I do? I got a gun!"

I heard someone say, "Take it easy, take it easy," and I hung up. They said they never got that second call. They say they responded to the first call in two minutes. But there were a lot of calls.

I call it fate. I think it was meant to happen, sometimes it's meant to happen. You go to work a certain way every day. One day you take a different street and then you get run over. If you hadn't taken that street, it wouldn't have happened. It's fate. It was meant to happen. Why were the cops so busy? They usually responded in minutes. This time they didn't. It was longer than usual. It was . . .

I tried to go out the front way. I looked out the window and there were more people there. I was crying. This is when I had that attack, it involved my head. It got boiling hot, just like somebody had taken their fist and put it in the back of your head. It was a real strange feeling. A psychiatrist said I had adrenaline shock. It just bombarded me with all that power.

What I did, I opened the door. They had run down the stairs. I followed them. I was in the doorway to the building. One of them had gone to the front and one of them had stayed at the edge of the driveway. The one who was at the driveway said, "Hey, he's out here. He's got a gun!" I brought the gun up and shot it in the air.

The lady in the second floor said I yelled, "Stop or I'll shoot," after the first shot, but I don't know if I said anything. He didn't stop. . . .

[The rest of this is said through tears:]

He grabbed his chest and went to his knees, then his head hit the ground. He was never . . . Oh, God! . . . he was in a kneeling position with his head down. The other guy was coming. I shot at his feet, because I had already hit someone and I couldn't believe it. I thought he was just playing funny, you know? I just didn't think . . . When I shot at the other guy's feet . . .

I go through this all the time, you know? I picture me firing the gun, it's at this angle, my hand is like this, I had the gun down and what it did, it hit the driveway and hit the guy in the head. He got hit by a lousy shot. It ricocheted into his head. So I brought it down and . . .

[Bob stopped talking for a while. When he was ready to continue:]

Then what happened?

I ran up to my apartment. I heard footsteps. I put more bullets in my gun. I hollered, "Who's there?"

They said, "The police."

I didn't believe it because I didn't hear a siren and it was such a long time for the cops to come. I looked, it was them. "Put the gun down." I came out. They put cuffs on and . . .

They said, "Couldn't you wait another minute? We were up the street."

I said, no.

I didn't realize . . . I didn't realize it had happened. I thought he was just wounded in the arm or something. I didn't know nothing about how he was. They took the cuffs off after I sort of calmed down. They let me change my clothes. I was brought to the police station and questioned. The state police came in, and the assistant DA came in and asked a lot of questions. I kept asking, "How's the guy doing? How's that guy doing?" They said they didn't know. Finally, the state police detective told me he was dead.

How did you feel when you heard that?

I was still in shock. I was very upset. Just talking about it makes me very upset now. I couldn't believe it. I must have turned white because the detective said, "Are you all right?" I couldn't believe it, that he was dead. I stayed there until four in the morning, then they let me go.

I tried to go back to work. Forget it. The boss looked at me. I only had a half hour's sleep. He said, "What happened to you? You must have had a helluva date over the weekend."

I said, "No, something happened to me."

He said, "Is it in the paper this morning?"

I said, "Yeah."

"You go home."

I stayed there three, four days. I tried to get back to work. I came out of the shock, but I couldn't function. I cried all the time, got the shakes. I threw up. I was really sick. I ended up in the hospital and I had to see a psychiatrist. After that night was over, I'd still lay there and hear the gunshot, the banging at the door . . .

The shooting was November 3. From November 3 until— what's today? April 10?—until April 10 I never got a good night's sleep. Four months is it?

Then there was the grand jury trial to go through. I would just think, "What are they going to do to me? What kind of people are going to be on the jury?" You know, you wonder about that.

I read the police report. One of them admitted to almost everything. The other two were covering up, the real punks.

My lawyer took me to the courthouse. I was supposed to be kept separate from the rest of them, but one of them was still in the courthouse hallway with his lawyer. But he kept his head down, he knew he had done wrong.

Then it was time to go in. Oh, God! When they opened that door . . . I thought it would be like a judge's room, with a table and all. Just thinking about it . . . because I hate crowds of people and there were a whole bunch of people in there, in a small room. I thought it wouldn't be like that.

The prosecutor had to question me about everything that led up to it, the history and how it escalated. Then the jury asked me questions. I didn't have my lawyer with me. I had to answer alone. I told them, I knew down deep that it was terrible to have done this, but I knew I was really protecting myself. I feared for my life. There's no question in my mind about it, even today.

They asked me all kinds of questions, how I held the gun, all of it. Then, of course, the last question, how I felt about having shot someone.

I broke down . . .

I had gone to the cemetery. I had made peace with the guy and I said what I had to say to him. I told him, "Your friends are saying it was all your idea to do this to me. You know better. You take care of it." And I was found not guilty. So. That was it . . .

What was it like to go to the cemetery?

It was something I had to do because I took someone's life. But, yet, they wanted to take my life too. I found out later that this guy was not one of the ones that had been bothering me for the past eight months. He was someone who had started it a couple days before. But I didn't know that. I mean . . . I thought he was one of the regulars. But he wasn't. He was the one who was up front. He was the bravest one. He was the one . . . see, those other guys stayed behind. He wanted to show his new friends that he could be the tough one and get me first. It didn't happen that way.

How long after the shooting did the grand jury meet?

They met December 11. About four weeks after the shooting. Then three weeks ago—the last part of March—the two guys came back. They threw smoke bombs in my window. I went down with my gun. I wasn't going to use it. I knew the cops would come and I just wanted to show the police that this was still a critical thing. These guys were not going to give up. The police tried to take the gun away from me, but I said, "I'm not going to use it. Tell those guys to leave me alone!"

But they couldn't catch them in front of my house, they'd run away, so they couldn't do anything. I called the state police, they couldn't do anything. I told the police, "What do you need? Another dead body before you do anything about this?" I couldn't get anywhere.

Then my landlord—he's seventy years old and scared—he asked me to leave. "For your peace of mind and mine," he said. "I want you to vacate the apartment." And he was almost in tears because he didn't want me to go. I'd been a good tenant, paid my rent all the time, never had any parties. I mean, I was an ideal tenant. But because of all this he asked me to leave.

I called my lawyer and he said, "Bob, I think it's better for you to leave."

So, I decided to go. I couldn't sleep at night until two or three in the morning. I was always looking out the window. There was more damage done around the house. So I left Lewiston.

I won't tell you where I am now. I moved to a new home, a new town. I've been here for three days and I've had sleep for three days and it's been solid sleep, not waking up two or three or four or five times, every time I hear a noise. I'm able to sleep, solidly. That makes a big difference. But it's still not home. It feels strange.

I hope nothing can hurt me here. Maybe I can function a little better, walk down the street and go to the store without any fear.

I've learned one thing. I'm never going to tell anyone that I'm here. People don't know, people in Lewiston, the general public. They don't know about me being here. I'm going to keep it that way. When people ask me, "Are you gay? Are you married?" whatever, I'm going to say, "Hey, I lead a quiet life, I haven't found the right girl yet, and that's it." I'm going to do that in order that I don't have to go through this again.

I'm never going to make friends. I'm just going to go to work, come home, watch TV, got to bed, that's it. It's very lonely. But I don't want to go through this again.

I'm going to lie from now on.

1986

LETTERS FROM MAINE

Preston worried that living so far from the main centers of gay activity and thought would cut him off from the contacts he had begun to develop as a writer. To maintain his place in the community of gay writers and thinkers, he determined to write for the small, local gay weeklies starting to be published in places like Boston, Miami, and Minneapolis.

Having worried that leaving the fast lane would deprive him of his material, he soon realized that this *was* his material. The mere fact of his being an openly gay writer in a state like Maine in 1979 was newsworthy. Preston's "Letters from Maine," eventually syndicated in many periodicals across the country, took the form of dispatches from the front lines. Energized by the grassroots activism that was cropping up throughout the state, he became a field correspondent whose self-appointed task was to inform lesbians and gay men in more urban areas that theirs was not the only gay world.

These brief articles, often written under deadline, represent Preston's writing in its most elemental, unpolished form. Their style may seem overly polemical now, but in the time and place in which he was operating, these arguments had not been heard before. Simply by treating gay issues as worthy of reporting, he was laying down the foundations of the just-emerging lesbian and gay community in Maine. A decade later, the articles document the tremendous advances accomplished by the gay and lesbian rights movement.

Most of the "Letters" deal with homophobic tragedies and issues of discrimination, but Preston also used the articles as a forum to describe Maine's weather, the change of seasons, and life in a small community. The "Letters" are invaluable snapshots of gay life in a particular time and place.

Summer Arrives in Maine

When people ask us why we stay here and don't move to some more comfortable climate, my friends and I usually respond with a volley of insistent statements about the wonders of the seasons. The constant reminder of rebirth and renewal that comes with spring, the joy of summer, and the beauty of fall—these are all factors attesting to the truth of the roadsigns when you enter the state: MAINE: THE WAY LIFE SHOULD BE.

The more hearty even claim to love the winter and look forward to the first snowfall, though I know at least one native who steals off to Boston in darkest February for "the warmth." (Boston is invariably ten degrees warmer than Portland.)

There are many changes that come with living in a region of such intense seasonal divergence. One peculiar to gay life here in Maine has to do with the slogan on our license plates: "Vacationland."

All of New England may be disrupted by the surge of aliens that descends on us in summer. But I think the gay community of Portland must suffer the greatest revolution of all. We are a small city of 60,000. Our life is slow and easy, our bondings close and communal.

Everything changes on Memorial Day.

For the most part the alterations are eagerly anticipated and humorously prepared for. Our sexual and relational possibilities explode from provincially small to seemingly inexhaustible. Men and women look forward to visits from urban friends whose reluctance even to write us in winter turns into frantic desire to visit—and to accept our offer of free lodging.

Many of us are especially anxious to prepare for new . . . ah . . . *friends*. We dream of Big Apple bodies on the beach and

Philadelphia torsos on the dance floor. We fantasize about latent lovers from Washington and new romances from Boston. We're even willing to make little compromises to meet some tourist expectations. Gene and I feel a particular need to hone our native New England accents, softened beyond recognition by Midwestern colleges. All winter we've gleefully congratulated one another when a natural "ayah" or an organic "caaaah" came from our lips.

Tourists, after all, love authentic Yankees, and if a hard vowel or a colorful phrase will please them, why not?

There's also a bittersweet edge to it all. I sometimes think of giving a temporary good-by party for some friends—the ones I know will be lost in the deluge.

Jamie's always a trusted companion and loyal mate during the off-season—the time of year when there aren't many tourists around. He's always there to share a beer or listen to a story. He always greets everyone with a loud heartfelt hello—until Memorial Day.

Then he goes into a strange reverse hibernation. He slinks in the shadows of the bars of Portland, lingers on the edge of the disco in Ogunquit, the nearby gay beach resort. He's on the prowl for visitors and we must forgive him. He is, after all, one of our major tourist attractions.

It will all work out. Just as Labor Day will inevitably arrive and just as the leaves will finally burst into brilliant foliage in autumn, so too will Jamie come back to us in October and we'll all settle back and enjoy one another and the intimacy of our small city and state.

Until next June.

1983

Life Is Different Here

"They really mean it when they say they'll call tomorrow!" That's a fairly common statement up here. You hear it from men who are experiencing gay life in a small city for the first time. There are many such men moving to Portland right now. A very few are returning to their childhood homes. I'm one of an equally small number who have chosen Portland because of our desire to move back to New England. We're not Mainers and have only a tenuous claim to the local Yankee identity; still, as natives of the region, we are more likely to understand the dynamics of life here. The people who have trouble are the ones who really are "from away"—the Yankee term for foreigners.

These men emigrate to Maine from New York and Philadelphia, from Florida and California. A few are trying to recapture memories of youthful vacations; others are escaping jobs and lifestyles that proved too pressured and too unfulfilling. Some arrive with a commitment to stay (we'll believe it after they've weathered a couple of winters); others simply want to spend their summers on the coast or in the mountains.

By coming to Portland, these men are by no means escaping gay life. Though it has a distinct small-town feel, Portland has all the other accoutrements of big city life that gay men are supposed to want: restaurants, theater, a symphony. It has bars populated with clones. In fact, the year-round gay community in Portland—augmented by the seasonal populations in the nearby resorts, especially Ogunquit—is often cited as the reason people relocate to this particular region.

And there's something else here that often seems lost in big city life: Romance.

The men of Portland want lovers. Forget your stereotypes: these men are not hopeless neurotics, nor are they irreparable bumpkins just because they think gayness does not have to equal singleness. They simply believe in relationships.

I sometimes hear comments to the effect that these guys are in Portland because they couldn't make it anywhere else. This is offensive and untrue. These are men who have chosen the small-town lifestyle, infused it with a healthy dose of gay awareness, and are going about the business of constructing a gay identity in their own context.

Someone who has lived in a big-city gay ghetto doesn't quite know how to deal with the scene here. He's used to saying, "Call me tomorrow," with about as much meaning as "Have a nice day." He has also probably come to think of having a lover as something akin to a virus: this too shall pass.

Gay life in Maine works from different premises. The men here place a premium on knowing and relating to the men they sleep with. Sure, you can find sex as anonymous as that in urban baths if you really want it: in the parks, the peeps, and turnpike rest areas. But that usually means doing it with straight-identified men whose hang-ups make them seldom worth the trouble.

Not that these gay men in Maine demand monogamy. Rather, they want a caring relationship. If that means you only want to be a fuck buddy, that's fine (especially in the off-season when no tourists are around). But you are expected to call the next morning, to find the time for long conversations in the bars, to come to dinner occasionally, to do more than nod when you pass on the street. What it boils down to is that you are expected to give other gay men some acknowledgment that you all belong to the same community.

After a while the newcomer settles into the local routine and learns to enjoy it. He'll still not be quite as ready to set up housekeeping as the locals, but the network of sexual relationships he develops will open new sets of possibilities. Friendliness, a lack of attitude, and communal support will become welcome ideals.

Even as he internalizes these small-town values, the former New Yorker will still occasionally get a glint in his eye after surveying the all-too-familiar faces of winter. A sense of wanderlust will take over as he recalls sexual escapades of the past. Finally, sometimes only in a whisper, he'll turn to his neighbor—the one who has also spent time in big-city gay life—and say, "Wouldn't you really like to go to the Mineshaft this weekend? I'll drive."

1983

Trouble in Paradise

Gay residents of the small beach resort town of Ogunquit, Maine, have begun to refer to their running battles with the village's straight bigots as their "rites of spring."

Last year the gays were on the offensive in Ogunquit. The seniors at neighboring Wells High School each had the opportunity to list in the yearbook those things they liked most and hated most. Fourteen of the ninety-four listed "fags," "queers," or "faggots" as the thing they couldn't stand.

The resulting uproar—complete with public apology from the high school principal, who tried to explain that the yearbook adviser was under the impression that the judgments were an expression of the students' right to freedom of speech—seemed to have many beneficial repercussions. Gays felt they had won some modicum of respect for having protested the outlandish student opinions; issues of homophobia were brought out into the open for all to see and discuss; and a basically gay organization, the Ogunquit Business Guild, was created to oversee gay issues in the community.

A counterattack was launched this year by those people who simply cannot tolerate a gay presence in town, even though Ogunquit has been known for decades as a gathering place for New England and Quebec gays. Apparently the issue isn't that gays shouldn't be in the community but, instead, that they shouldn't be so obvious.

Ogunquit's commercial life is utterly dependent upon gay tourists. As more and more gay people have sought out gay resorts for their vacations and weekends, the village's reputation has spread. Gay businesses—bars and guesthouses especially—have boomed. In what should be seen as a natural progression, those establishments have sought publicity and have advertised in gay periodicals.

It seems that the idea of "our" gays having a discreetly quiet time was something that Ogunquit's other residents could swallow. But the concept of those same gay people seeking to attract others was anathema.

The issue of just what kind of gays should be "allowed" into Ogunquit began to simmer in April when a motorcycle club from Rhode Island held its annual run in town. A fistfight broke out between one club member and an adolescent who had taunted him. The image of dozens of beleathered men on the streets of the village appalled some residents.

A lightning rod for the antagonism presented itself when articles on Ogunquit were published in one national gay magazine and a number of regional gay publications. Straights had already been complaining that some of Ogunquit's gay bars and guesthouses had been advertising in New England's gay press when a column in *Limelight*, a Boston-based bar throwaway, mentioned "drugs, drugs, drugs, sex, sex, sex" in the same article that it mentioned the seasonal opening of three Ogunquit bars.

But the premier issue of *Torso*, a new gay porn glossy, was the real rallying point. Here was a nationally circulated magazine, generously laden with nude photographs, telling the gay world that Ogunquit was "a booming gay village." (A moment of journalistic integrity: for the record, I wrote the *Torso* article. It was a piece of tourist fluff—where to go and what to do. It did not encourage any actions that would have violated village or state laws and, in fact, warned that at night the beach had been the scene of violent attacks on gay men.)

An organization called Integrity for Ogunquit was formed to counteract the publicity (its founders apparently missing the irony that Integrity is also the name of the gay Episcopal network, one of the largest gay organizations in the country). Integrity's leaders seemed to assume that the mere threat of retaliation would be sufficient to make all involved back down and resume our proper, subservient ethic: Spend money and don't make a spectacle of yourself.

When some of the gays refused, citing the obvious fact that to them Ogunquit *was* a "booming gay village," the undertakings got vicious. Only two men had been named in the *Torso* article, Tom Corbett and Tom St. John, real estate agents employed by the local Century 21 office, which also has an insurance agency attached to it. The (antigay) Integrity members threatened to organize a boycott of the insurance business if Corbett and St. John remained with the realty office. On May 14 the two men were called in by manager Michael Kucsma and told that their contracts had been terminated.

It was at this point that the Portland media picked up the story. York County bureau chief Shelly Murphy of the *Portland Press-Herald* acknowledged that the firing of the men—the fact that people were losing their livelihood over the issue—made the controversy fodder for the press.

The appearance of major articles in the *Press-Herald* escalated the conflict. On one front the media attention further infuriated the antigay straights. Their feeling about town issues is largely that they should remain quiet and "inside the family." Their calm was especially ruptured when reports of the firings began airing on television.

On the other front, the reports also galvanized the gays and their supporters. Kucsma had fired the men to save the insurance business, but, while saving himself from an Integrity-sponsored boycott, he discovered a long line of clients at his door who'd come to take away their business in support of the dismissed men. Kucsma, clearly losing on every side, refused further comment to the press. The agency's offices were closed and signs removed.

On Saturday, May 15, town officials, including the three selectmen, the fire chief, and the police chief, met in a closed-door session to discuss the issues. Their stance was captured in a quotation given by Town Manager Robert Brown to the *Press-Herald*: "I don't know how to deal with that article [in *Torso*]. . . . As far as I'm concerned it's not a gay or an antigay issue. All we deal with is the problems of the town, [and] whether people are gay or straight is irrelevant. I think we have a problem with drug and alcohol abuse in [Ogunquit], but not just in [the gay] community."

The attempt to defuse the idea of a gay issue in Ogunquit was betrayed by actions of the police over that weekend. Uniformed officers began making regular inspections of the premises of gay businesses. Building code enforcers made outrageously thorough searches of gay establishments, obviously hoping to find fire or building code violations that would justify closing them. None were found.

Don't queers run away from police? Don't they disappear at the sight of a uniform? No one can take the heat from being identified as gay, right? The police have found that some of the rules of gay life have changed in recent years.

The gay bar owners have come up with a unified policy. When policemen walk into one of the discos, all the lights are to be turned up and the patrons, bartenders, and owners are to surround the officers and pepper them with questions. Why are you here? What do you want? The reply—usually that they're looking for minors—is jeered. The policemen are, to say the least, embarrassed by the attention.

Bar business in Ogunquit, especially in springtime, is heavily dependent on day trippers from cities such as Portland and, most importantly, Boston. Ogunquit is less than an hour and a half drive from that metropolis and its location (half the driving distance from Boston of competing gay resort Provincetown) is its main reason for off-season success. The antigay straights found that, rather than frightening patrons away, the controversy attracted people who wanted to support the local community.

This was especially true of gay people from Portland. That

city and Ogunquit form the core of Maine's openly gay population, and, as one Portlander told me, "Things like this make
me so fucking mad that I have to do *something*. The least I can
do is drive down there and talk to people and make sure they
know we're all still here."

Corbett and St. John have hired an attorney to investigate
their own legal remedies. (As a result of their attorney's advice
they're no longer talking to the press either.) The Ogunquit
Business Guild's attorney is also investigating possible violations of the state's "sunshine laws" prohibiting closed meetings
of town officials.

The publisher of *Torso*, fueled by a combination of honest
concern and the opportunity to publicize his new magazine, is
pursuing action at a national level. Especially fascinated by the
overtness of the antigay job discrimination, he is having his
magazine's lawyers approach the national headquarters of Century 21 to attempt to persuade them to take some action.

It is, of course, the human element of two people losing
their jobs that makes the situation more than a simple case of
intra-community squabbling in a small resort town. Here is
one of the most up-front forms of discrimination to be found:
two highly successful professional men (Corbett was the top
commercial real estate broker in the state for Century 21 in
four of his fifteen months of employment) who have been fired
for no other apparent reason than that their names were mentioned in a gay magazine.

As Corbett told the *Press-Herald*: "We are not leaving Ogunquit. We will survive and we will be successful. We have been
successful because we are honest, efficient, hard workers and it
has nothing to do with our sexual preference."

There is as of yet no indication that the summer season in
Ogunquit will be anything less than spectacular for the gay
tourist trade. No reservations have been canceled as a result of
the controversy, and the gay businesses in town have given no
hint of closeting themselves.

The rules of politics are constantly changing. While the controversy was brewing in Ogunquit, the Maine Democratic Party Convention was meeting in Portland, forty miles to the north. The party platform included a gay rights plank, and party candidates can now expect to be questioned about their stand on gay rights.

The gay people of Ogunquit knew the political winds were changing. Evidently some of the straights didn't.

1982

A Question of Survival

Milo, Maine, seems a strange place for a gay rights battle. But people, circumstances, and coincidence have brought it about.

Terry Wallace, a thirty-eight-year-old gay man, has been fired from the Three Rivers Ambulance Company, where he had worked as an Emergency Medical Technician (EMT). He was charged with drinking on the job, "flaunting his penis" at women, and offering himself sexually to his male co-workers with "dirty words."

This tiny community 48 miles north of Bangor, over 150 miles north of Portland, evidently didn't question the rightness of the decision to take Terry Wallace's job away from him. Sworn statements from co-workers denying the allegations of drinking and sexual harassment were ignored. They could be, since everyone in town knew Wallace was gay. He had come out openly more than ten years ago after his divorce from a hometown girl.

Often gay people don't fight for their jobs when they lose them. I know one man here in Portland who was fired from a local restaurant for being too "flagrantly" gay. It wasn't worth it to him to challenge the place. The waiter's job was a convenience of the moment for him, and he could find plenty of others like it. The people involved weren't important to him, not important enough even to acknowledge them as worthy opponents.

But for Terry Wallace the EMT job was a question of survival. The grinding poverty of rural Maine is something seldom seen by tourists. Those who spend time in Ogunquit, Kennebunkport, or Portland probably wonder how it's possible that this state is always listed as one of the poorest in the country. A few hours driving over the backroads away from the ocean beaches, roads lined with shacks and old mobile homes, will tell you.

There is a brutality to the poverty of Maine. The weather helps bring it on—that and the lack of employment. Many things that might seem romantic are necessities here. Do you like the idea of Terry Wallace building himself a log cabin in the woods? He didn't do it for the sake of romance. It was the only way he could have a house to live in; it was much cheaper than renting an apartment.

Think it's noble to heat that house with wood? You probably wouldn't if you had to do it year-round because there was no other way to provide heat. Hauling wood in the brisk fall air sounds good and manly; it loses it appeal when you have to do it in subzero temperatures.

There's almost no industry in the area around Milo. Certainly no industry that's hiring. And Terry Wallace needed that job.

He might have given up and moved somewhere more tolerant—New York, perhaps, where he'd lived briefly ten years earlier, pursuing an acting career. But his father had a heart attack two and a half years ago. His mother was alone. His parents—living off a retirement pension—needed him.

The pull of family can be intense. For Terry it was powerful enough to bring him back to Milo in an instant, without hesitation. Ask him if he should have made the move—left the security of the gay ghetto and the excitement of limousines and cast parties—and he'll look at you blankly. He had no choice.

The EMT job was the only one he could get that would pay his way. It's a piecework job. EMTs are paid for each ambulance run they make—so much per run. In the world of Milo, Maine, this job was lucrative.

While many of our legal battles are carefully chosen fights designed as much for publicity and political impact as for pro-

tection of an individual, in some, such as this one, the partici-
pant is acting from the most fundamental position of self-
protection.

Terry Wallace is now surviving on odd jobs—often he's paid
in barter rather than cash, that's part of the poverty of rural
New England—and it's not enough. That job with Three Rivers Ambulance Company was his salvation. He wants it back
and he *needs* it back. He's going to court.

The National Gay Task Force referred him to a lawyer in
Machias, Ronald Close, who's agreed to take the case, if Wallace can come up with $750 for court costs and other minimal
expenses.

Wallace is hitchhiking across the state to raise the money.
He's doing it a little desperately right now. The phone company's on his back and he's afraid the plug will be pulled and
he'll be unable to communicate with others in the state who
are trying to help him.

Interweave, a statewide group composed mostly of Unitarian gay men and lesbians, has sent out an appeal and has received about $80. Cycles, a bar in Portland, threw a fund-raiser
that netted $175. Wallace is hoping there will be more.

The real funding is probably going to come from his unemployment checks. He hopes to receive a group of them all at
once when his claim is finally processed. He has food stamps
for sustenance and intends to use the unemployment to make
up the difference for the lawyer's bill.

Talking to Wallace over coffee one morning I questioned
him more fully about living in Maine. We each talked about
New York and our experiences there. We each had felt similar
pulls back to New England.

"Where I live," he told me, "is like a man's dream. It's beautiful." He went on and tied his experience growing up in Milo
to his acting career. "I played in *Spoon River Anthology* once.
There's a character in it, Willy Metcalfe, who's something of a
dullard, sort of dumb, but who sleeps in the barn with the

horses. It was the one role I ever had that I instinctively knew. When I was a kid I had a horse and I would sleep in her manger, just so I could listen to her chewing the hay while I went to sleep."

I wondered about those kinds of memories. I examined some of my own prejudices. My immediate response was that a man like Wallace should have returned to New York or at least Portland, where he wouldn't have to submit to the humiliations being heaped on him in Milo. But what kind of blind submission is that, to assume the ghetto is where we have to go? Why do we let people tell us where we can and can't live?

The isolation is probably the worst part about being gay in a small town. It's all the worse for Wallace in the middle of this fight. "No matter how strong you are," he explained, "you can only take so much when you're alone. If there was someone there with me it'd be a different story."

But the pull of family is too strong to allow him the easy option of leaving. Wallace's father had another heart attack a few months ago. He would have died if Terry hadn't been there—and if Terry hadn't had his EMT training, which he used to save his father's life.

1983

A Murder in Maine

There have been insidious speculations that somehow Charles O. Howard may have invited his own murder. Any attempt to blame the victim of this outrageous crime must be instantly dismissed.

To wear an earring on the street does not justify execution.

To appear to be less than perfectly masculine does not rationalize killing.

To walk a city's streets in the evening is not a reason for assassination.

That is all Charlie had done: he wore an earring, appeared effeminate, walked a city's streets. For those simple reasons the police tell us he was chased through Bangor, kicked, beaten, and then thrown into a river as he pleaded with his assailants that he could not swim.

The event did not happen in a vacuum. I wonder if the young men allegedly involved had heard members of the state legislature as they stood in the House and Senate and described gay men and lesbians as less than human.

I wonder if they went to church services where religious leaders dismissed the humanity of gay men and lesbians.

I wonder if they knew that the most basic human rights— to rent an apartment, to hold a job, to live in safety—have too often been denied gay men and lesbians.

I wonder who told them it was all right to kill a gay man?

We must judge our society by the most essential standard of civilization: Is human life protected? The murder of Charles Howard makes us question just what is the status of human life in Maine. Is there a sliding scale to the importance of human life? Is it less horrible if a gay man is killed than another person? Are human rights expendable at the whim of a street gang? Do our laws have sufficient strength to insure all citizens of Maine the right to preserve our own lives?

We here in Portland are more than usually secure, so we must always remember that we are the exception to the rule too often found outside this city. This cruel and horrible act must remind our gay community that our privileges are just that—exceptions. Our relative freedom here must be constantly guarded and defended. If the need for a statewide gay rights bill was ever in doubt, if anyone thought the demand for this extension of basic human rights legislation was trivial— the memory of Charlie Howard stands as a harsh refutation. We must not forget that our rights—even the most fundamental—can be snatched away by bigots.

The crime committed against Charlie must become part of the gay men and lesbians of Maine. We must realize that if we do not insist upon our own dignity, if we don't demand equal protection under the law, if we don't prosecute when our rights are transgressed, then we are inviting on ourselves the fate that befell Charlie.

Charlie Howard should not have died at the age of twenty-three. This young man, who we are told was a compassionate and tender soul, should never have been murdered. The only greater crime would be if we allow his death to go unnoticed.

Gay rights are not trivial when they mean the preservation of human life. Gay rights are not to be dismissed when they support the dignity of human existence.

We must all call on our political leaders to stand up and be counted. The attorney general's office must immediately call for the prosecution of the alleged murderers as adults; they should not receive the protection of juveniles. A message must be sent to all other people in the state: *This will not be tolerated.*

But this event did not happen in a vacuum, and the response to it must not either. Every state official, educator, religious leader, member of the media, and anyone else involved in shaping the image of humanity that we hold must come to grips with the ways that homophobia—the blind hatred of gay men and lesbians—permeates our society.

And we—gay men and lesbians—must begin to insist more adamantly on these essential values, these moral imperatives: We must not hide, refusing to risk involvement by not reporting crimes against us or refusing to allow the state's leaders to forget just how much a part of society we are.

Too many people were involved in Charlie Howard's death. Let's hope at least as many people will become involved in his lasting memory.

1984

Tolerance Day

The saga played out in Madison, Maine, this past January isn't one of the most pleasant chapters in the history of gay politics. At one level, it must be seen as a major defeat. But there are also ways in which it was an important victory.

Last summer's murder of Charlie Howard in Bangor has, understandably, made people aware of the effects of prejudice in this state. When the students at Madison High School came back to classes after their summer vacation, the tragedy was one of the most pressing items they wanted to discuss with their social science teacher, David Solmitz.

Solmitz encouraged the students' discussion and suggested they broaden their inquiry to investigate all forms of intolerance. What is the cost of society's various manifestations of bigotry? What are the roots?

The topics caught the students' attention, and Solmitz decided to work with that interest. He devised a day-long program, to be called Tolerance Day, during which the victims of societal abuse would come and talk about their experiences to the teenagers.

Like many other small towns in New England, Madison is virtually homogenous in its class and racial makeup. It's very possible, for instance, that a kid could grow up in such a town and never meet a black person or a Latino. Solmitz knew he was going to have to start at square one in setting up his Tolerance Day. Nothing could be taken for granted. He brought together a group of representatives from various minority groups, including a black, a Jew, an ex-convict, an American Indian, an elderly person, a veteran, a high school dropout, two handicapped people . . . and a lesbian.

The lesbian was Dale McCormick, president of the Maine Lesbian/Gay Political Alliance. McCormick is a delight, a disarming speaker and a bright and witty presence. She's also proven her ability to get things done. In addition to helping form the Alliance, she was elected a delegate to the national Democratic Party Convention in San Francisco.

McCormick thought the opportunity to talk to the Madison High School students was an especially important one. These kids were the same age and background as the Bangor teenagers who had killed Charlie Howard. She felt a need to reach them, to display humanity in the person of a homosexual.

But the members of the Kennebec Valley Grange didn't think her appearance was a good thing at all. They called an emergency meeting. All the members of Madison's clergy showed up to support the Grange members who wanted to cancel the visit by the homosexual leader. They pressured the local school board, and the board finally caved in. All others could come to Madison's Tolerance Day, they decreed, but not McCormick.

Things happened quickly after that. McCormick, declaring that her right to free speech had been infringed, contacted the Maine Civil Liberties Union and took the school board to court. The media lunged at the story. It was front-page news throughout Maine as well as a major story for the national media. *USA Today*, the *Boston Globe*, and the wire services jumped on the tale of a rural school district deciding that there were limits to what could be tolerated, even on Tolerance Day.

The case was heard before Superior Court Justice Donald G. Alexander, who recognized the horrible events in Madison for what they were. He declared: "When the power of government sides with the voices of intolerance, it is a mighty force indeed."

Indeed it is. But it's one that cannot be denied. Justice Alexander went on to rule that "no matter how grievous the wrong that has been committed," since the wrong was directed at a lesbian, there was no legal recourse. There is, he explained, no protection of rights in the state of Maine for any gay man or lesbian.

"Courts are not legislatures," he went on to say. "We are not free to act every time that someone complains and we find that the public interest justifies action."

Dale McCormick did not go to Madison High School. The final appeal, to the chief justice of the Maine Supreme Court, was denied.

On the face of it, this is a great and mighty defeat. There is no way to get around the bleak fact that McCormick was denied her chance to speak to a group of teenagers who wanted to hear her.

But the overall impact of the decision has been surprisingly positive. It's hard to communicate to people outside of Maine just how much the death of Charlie Howard altered the way in which gay people and gay issues are discussed here. The media, for one thing, went through a crash course in sensitivity. The protest marches and expressions of our rage in all the large cities in Maine were spontaneous and loud declarations that gay rights is no longer a trivial issue.

With a state—an entire *state*—on edge over that incident and its repercussions, the idea of a small-town school board acting in such a Babbitish manner horrified many people. Whatever the limits of acceptable intolerance in our society when it comes to gay people, the Madison school board had gone beyond them so far as the media was concerned.

The *Portland Press-Herald*, in an unusual move, printed an editorial immediately in support of McCormick and chastising the Madison officials. Main Public Broadcasting devoted a special edition of its "Statewide" program to an interview with McCormick and Solmitz that included a segment with an embarrassingly inarticulate member of the Kennebec Valley Grange.

This media attention and the manner in which it presented

gay rights as a legitimate civil rights concern have had far more impact than a single day in a high school auditorium could have had. McCormick's sincerity and articulateness came across wonderfully on the television screen and in newspaper and radio interviews. If she had tried to create a better forum for herself and her views, she couldn't have.

The real shocker in the story, for many people, is the court decision. Justice Alexander's declaration that gay people exist without *any* constitutional protection has stunned people. It's always been easy for straights to claim that there is no need for a gay civil rights bill. The last time such a bill was presented to the state legislature, for example, one of the strongest arguing points against it was that it would be wasted energy, because gay people's rights were already covered.

That's not going to hold water now.

The same argument was used by a lot of gay men and women who were uneasy with the movement's leadership making too many waves. "Why bother?" they asked. "We're citizens. We don't need a special bill." Justice Alexander shot a gaping hole in that argument.

Throughout the entire incident, I read the newspapers and cheered Dale McCormick on. She has to be one of the most charming personalities we've come up with in the gay movement. In the middle of all the stress, she created what I would suggest as the new rallying cry for gay liberation. Trying to explain to a *Boston Globe* reporter why it was so important for the Madison students to see a gay person up close and personal, she told him, "I want them to see we're just like other people. . . . *We buy Girl Scout cookies!*"

Even during a disaster, McCormick can always come up with a good line. We can only hope her message is getting through to those kids who are so used to hearing the message of intolerance, even on Tolerance Day.

1985

Charlie's Day

Would it be possible for any of your members and friends on July 7 to do a Candlelight Service or march to "That Bridge"? Could you throw flowers into the River? Charlie so loved flowers and plants. If possible, please throw a single white rose with baby's breath and fern—tied with two ribbons—one of lavender and one of white.

Please, this would be a token to represent me for him—Then any other flowers from anyone else.

Excerpt from a letter to the
Bangor Unitarian Church
from Charlie Howard's mother

Nearly three hundred people marched through the streets of Bangor on July 7 in memory of the murder of Charlie Howard. On that date last year, three teenaged boys, driving through the city on a Saturday night, pulled up, leaving their female dates in the car, and chased Charlie and a friend down State Street. Charlie tripped; they caught him. Ignoring his pleas that he could not swim, these children of middle-class Bangor families, supposedly enraged by the sight of the known homosexual, tossed Charlie over the railing, after beating him and kicking his head. He drowned.

For many people, the idea that a young man could be murdered simply because he was gay became proof of the violence that is constantly directed toward us. That this country seethes with intolerance was proven, yet again, by the taunts of passing motorcyclists and others who saw the march this year: "Faggots!" "Queers!"

But to focus exclusively on the real intolerance of Bangor

and the countless numbers of other communities like it is to overlook the astonishing fact of the march. It had been planned long before the letter from Charlie's mother arrived at the Unitarian church. In fact, it has always been assumed that there would be a memorial for Charlie Howard.

That there is a community that defies the forces of ignorance and insists a person like Charlie be remembered is possibly the most impressive proof of the advance of gay activism in this country. There have been hundreds of Charlie Howards— and thousands more who will never be identified. Young men tormented into suicide in New Hampshire, lonely men tortured and murdered on the streets of Boston, men left to die on the sides of highways all through New England.

As I stood and watched the flowers fall down from the State Street bridge and float past the mourners who'd gathered there to pay their respects to this young man, I wondered just what he would have thought of all this. He had become a martyr. Who would ever choose to be that? But if the choice isn't ours . . .

> If that ever happened to me you're damn right I'd want people to use it! If I have to die, let my death have some meaning!
>
> *A gay man from Portland*

As our lives as gay people have been seen as trivial, so our deaths have been ignored. Until now. With roses and carnations, ferns and baby's breath, the people standing on the bridge faced the television cameras, withstood a collection of photographers, and came out of their closets to affirm that Charlie Howard was worth remembering.

The city of Bangor is still ruptured by the murder, a violent death that has never been seen as something that "happened here." But it did. And with it came the publicity. The town leaders chafe at the headline that doesn't seem to go away: "A City and Its Shame."

The officials still attempt to portray the murder as an isolated event, nothing to do with the social climate of Paul Bunyon's city, nothing to do with a lack of education in the schools, nothing to do with the only daily newspaper's constant battle against gay rights legislation, nothing to do with . . .

There are attempts at healing in the city. The Unitarian church to which Charlie had belonged recently called a gay man to its pulpit. The new pastor, Jay Deacon, says he'll never know just how much the trauma of Charlie's death had to do with the parish decision to hire him. But at least they aren't saying it had *nothing to do with* . . .

After the march, the crowd gathered at the church. There were small remembrances of Charlie. A hat was passed to help his mother pay the still outstanding funeral costs. She'd talked about the debt in her letter, that and the threats made against her life and the lives of her family members in their New Hampshire towns; ignorance has no special claim on Bangor. There were songs of resistance and there were songs of sorrow.

William Sloan Coffin, a fixture in the movement for civil justice in this country, also spoke. His schedule is constantly stretched by this movement, he told the crowd, demands are constantly being made, but he *had* to come to Bangor. You do not need to be gay to know that *attention must be paid.*

Coffin preached his themes of human respect, and he called Charlie a "son of America," a phrase President Reagan had used recently to describe a young sailor murdered in a Beirut hijacking. It was a good phrase, Coffin said. It was one that Charlie had the right to claim as much as any other victim of terrorism. And that, in the end, is what Charlie was—a victim of terrorists who would paralyze a whole segment of society with their threats of violence and arbitrary punishment.

How can we stop them?

By remembering. By remembering each and every July 7 from now till the end, till the end of the horror and the end of the forces that would deny a twenty-three-year-old man his life—only because he was gay.

1985

Jerry Falwell's Coming!

The leader of the Moral Majority is coming to Maine—and no one could be happier than the gay community.

It might seem strange, after taking endless abuse from Falwell and having to fight off his message of hate and prejudice for so many years, that any state's gays would be happy to know that he's targeted them for special treatment.

But old Jerry's not coming to Maine for the usual reasons. It's not likely this is going to be one of his major media events. He's coming to Maine to try to salvage what he can out of one of the religious right's most embarrassing moments in recent years.

Buddy Franklin is the reason for Falwell's pilgrimage to the Pine Tree State. Franklin was once such a powerful force in Maine politics that he convinced his old classmate—Falwell and Franklin graduated from the same bible college—there was no need for the Moral Majority here. He assured Falwell that he would take care of the Good Fight for The Cause. Maine was, as a result, the only state in the nation without a Moral Majority chapter.

Franklin's power base was the Bangor Baptist Church, the largest single fundamentalist congregation in New England. Franklin was the most articulate proponent of the religious right in the state. And that meant he was the most articulate opponent of gay rights. In fact, Franklin first came to statewide public notice with his ferocious attacks on the University of Maine when that institution officially recognized the gay and lesbian Wilde-Stein Club.

But a few months ago, Franklin's house came tumbling down. In a tearful press conference, the leader of the state's fundamentalist community admitted he had committed adultery. Rumor has it that Franklin's amour was a church organist. She allegedly made audio tapes of their trysts, and when Franklin tried to end the relationship, she threatened to hand them over to local television and radio stations. The tapes were never played, but that didn't stop the Maine media from having a field day with the story of the great moral judge falling in such a human fashion.

The public was able to watch the disintegration of the state's largest religious institution. Franklin's Bangor Baptist parish split into numerous small churches. The building was left nearly empty; where once there were thousands of regular worshipers, now there were only a few hundred. The church school, one of Franklin's major successes, was devastated by the resignation of faculty who felt betrayed by Franklin's revelations.

The coalition of the religious right in the state fell to pieces. Its other main figure, Jasper Wyman of the Maine Christian Civic League, inelegantly backed away from any association with his former ally, claiming the movement wouldn't be harmed by the "self-destruction" of one pillar. But Franklin had not been simply a part of the structure of Maine's right wing; he had been its foundation.

The only hope seemed to be Falwell. First of all, he was apparently the only person to whom Franklin would finally hand over control of the church. He was also seen as a charismatic leader who could heal the very real hurts of the community.

Falwell began by making every mistake possible. It may be that Falwell's native South accepts church-as-big-business, but that's unseemly in New England, where religion is supposed to be a very private affair. So it didn't go over well when the first evidence of the Falwell takeover of Bangor Baptist was the highly publicized arrival of the Moral Majority accountants. Dale McCormick, president of the Maine Lesbian/Gay Political Alliance, isn't the only liberal leader who had a hard time containing her joy over the right wing's problems. The televised pictures of three-piece-suited businessmen attempting to resuscitate what was once the major source of conservative political money in Maine was payoff for all the years of abuse the MLGPA had endured. McCormick says, "My first reaction was reveling in Franklin's having been caught in his hypocrisy. His politics have always been based on moral judgment. If that's your platform, then you had better be ready to live in a glass house."

Franklin wasn't.

The right wing isn't dead because of this affair. Wyman's Christian Civic League was recently able to meet the deadline to force a state referendum in favor of a draconian bill to limit obscenity in the state. But while such a petition drive would have been a piece of cake if Franklin's organization had been intact, Wyman's organization was barely able to meet the minimal requirements. The referendum is still far from probable victory; not only is there now noticeably less enthusiasm for any part of the right wing's agenda, there is a highly organized opposition.

"They're ebbing, you can feel it," McCormick says of the Christian right in Maine. "Their time has passed."

1986

Christmas 1983

The first snowfall.

We've waited a long time for it. November was the wettest month on record here—ever. Rain fell promiscuously and we all walked around in awe, thoroughly conscious that all of it could have been snow.

When the storm finally did come, the city erupted in spontaneous celebration. The hunks in the bars dragged their potential tricks out into the snowbanks to make angels; men walked in groups on the city's streets and sang; a bar played the Christmas tape by the Oak Ridge Boys and a howl of laughter came from the crowd when "Silent Night" was heard for the first time this year.

You have to celebrate the first snowfall. It will, after all, be *very* tired in February.

Snow brings subtle changes. This final proof that the tourists are gone alters how we all treat one another. We lose our facade of urbanity. In summer, Portlanders act under the pretense that this is a large city; in winter we realize we are a small town.

We become more internal. Solitude becomes more a companion. That and one another. There's more care here. The kind of touching and concern that would mark a New England village, not an American metropolis.

Winter's a time for us to listen more carefully to one another. I love the nights in the bars here now, when men who in summer had only seen one another across disco floors or near naked on the beach take the time to talk. The stories come out, the histories are given.

There's a reclaiming of friendships that have been loosened

too much by the summer. People come back into the warmth of Portland from the smaller resort communities. Norman's back from Ogunquit; Peter returned from Bar Harbor.

Holiday invitations arrive in the mail and it's nice to see that someone remembered you. More greetings are exchanged with men you saw last night at the cruise bar, at the pub. Every year it seems a little less like a membership in a hidden fraternity; every year it feels more like a community.

Everyone seems to have more time now. Everyone seems to need each other more. It's more common for the doorbell to ring unexpectedly, for someone to finally take you up on that offer to drop by for a cup of coffee.

Conversations in the winter are slower. People read more. They want to talk about a story or a book. They want to just sit with a friend and chat.

Everyone always wants to know how people can live in Maine in winter. There's a favorite T-shirt here: "If you can't take the winter, you don't deserve the summer." Perhaps that level of Puritan ethic still has a grasp on our beings. There's a sense of solidarity about the men who stay here year round—a kind of shared sense of surviving winter together. We become more aware of why we choose to live here.

Some of us came to Portland because it was the smallest city we could live in. That's my motivation. I need the amenities of an urban area, the resources, the gathering of people. Others are here because it's the largest city they can tolerate. Anything more becomes a jungle.

Whatever our respective motivations, we have a shared feeling, one that colors all our perceptions of this place and one another. There's something glorious about it. Almost everyone is where he wants to be.

With the first snow we draw together. Every year the motion is a little stronger, every year the results a little more comforting. Sure, there are faults, there are problems, there is always some element of discontent.

But most of all there's a sense of things working themselves out. The snow dampens the city noises; the cold forces us indoors. Another year is passing and most of us are still here; more have joined us. I have that feeling again it will be a good year.

1983

SOME OF US ARE DYING

John Preston had many identities throughout his life, and he learned to embrace many labels to describe himself: New Englander, writer, pornographer, person with AIDS. But he refused to view these identities separately. Each was part and parcel of the others.

He was particularly determined not to let himself be consumed by his identity as a person with AIDS. By no means did he avoid the topic, or his own diagnosis: he edited *Personal Dispatches: Writers Confront AIDS*; he authored two books about safe sex; he was on the board of directors of the AIDS Project of Southern Maine; he spoke and wrote actively about the need for greater awareness of the disease. But Preston refused to be defined by AIDS, and he rarely wrote about the disease for its own sake. Rather, he used AIDS to investigate larger issues: community, individual and group responsibility, the transformative power of storytelling. Andrew Holleran has written, "I always admired John for having HIV but never making it into his Main Topic, or Theme. He wanted to give it as little space as possible, I think, because he saw that life was much more fun and in a sense HIV had *nothing* to do with gayness."

Preston had left New York just before that city became the vortex of the disease, and he believed for a while that moving to New England had literally saved him from infection. Of course this was not the case; viruses do not honor state boundaries, and Preston's frequent trips back to New York provided ample opportunity for infection. He was diagnosed as HIV-positive in 1986.

Living in Maine could not keep Preston's body from getting sick, but it did eventually save him. By seeing himself in terms of the communal traditions of New England, he was able to accept that his own death, as his life, could be a contribution to a larger history. As he told an interviewer some six months before he died, "What I finally had to understand was that I was only a chapter in the narrative. It went on before me and it would go on afterward. At that point, being a part of the truly glorious history of New England became one of my major sources of support. One came into the world, one made one's contributions, and one moved out. And I was liberated from that moment on."

I have included in this section Preston's AIDS writings that speak most deeply of his New England context. The essays show a progression of awareness and involvement: from the first piece he wrote about AIDS, warning people in Maine before there were any diagnosed cases of HIV infection in the state; through his response to his own infection; into serious investigations of the role of the writer in a community devastated by plague; and finally his last public message about AIDS to the Portland community.

Some of Us Are Dying

"Some of Us Are Dying" is the first significant piece Preston wrote addressing AIDS. Written in 1983, the essay now seems raw, but it stands as a crucial piece of history, in terms of both Preston's development as a writer/activist and the course of the epidemic itself.

Preston's perspective is especially noteworthy because, living in Maine, he had the opportunity to address a captive population *before* the epidemic had touched them directly. At the time he was writing, as he notes, there had not yet been a single "native" case of AIDS diagnosed in the entire state of Maine.

The very notion of "native" cases of AIDS seems oddly parochial in the context of the worldwide AIDS pandemic as we now know it. But the attitude of separation into native and nonnative, us and them, was a force Preston understood to be all too prevalent in Maine, a state where everyone not born within its borders is marked permanently as being "from away." In "Some of Us Are Dying," Preston argues forcefully for the need to transcend such distinctions.

Ntozake Shange has written about the "havoc wrought on the souls of people who aren't supposed to exist." We gay people know that well.

We've each had to go through the same essential dynamic:

We discovered our sexuality in isolation.

We learned to hate our sexuality.

We lived with our self-hatred.

We discovered our sexuality as members of a heterosexual

society—usually in our own heterosexual family. There were no socially sanctioned lifestyles for us to fit into. The strength to defy what America called "healthy" was difficult—at first impossible—for us to find.

This sexual identity that everyone else seemed to hate could only be hated by us as well. It was a dark inner secret that had to be hidden, had to be suppressed if we were to continue living.

The burden of strangling a part of ourselves inextricably led to a general sense of self-hatred. How could this being who had such a loathsome secret be anything but hideous?

These personal judgments were expanded to include others. Our special condemnation was reserved for other gay people, especially those who dared to exhibit the telltale characteristics we so desperately tried not to show. Who is ever more vicious to a queen or a butch or a clone than a closeted homosexual?

If we were unable to break this pattern of judgment we ended any hope for our lives. The person who hates his or her self cannot love. That person cannot form healthy relationships. That person cannot help but smother in hypocrisy and loneliness; that person often can find relief only in drugs or alcohol or perhaps too inevitably in suicide.

How each of us found the courage and the strength to end that process of self-denial is beyond my ability to comprehend. How each of us refused to accept the havoc of society's condemnation is a victory of the soul equal to any other I know.

We usually term that salvation of self "coming out." But during my first months in Maine, on a winter night a few years ago in a house on the water not far from Portland, a group of gay men used a much better phrase. After dinner, eight of us sat in a circle. Calm in one another's acceptance we talked about our lives since we had *come to our senses*.

Coming to our senses began—or so it seemed from each of our stories—by saying no to whatever it was that had kept us from self-affirmation. We decided our souls were too valuable to be ruled by havoc. We insisted on their wholeness and even beauty.

The immensity of each person's struggle to come to his senses should have been more than enough for anyone to experience in a lifetime. But we also had to learn that one does not exist in a vacuum.

Ten years ago a group of people met at the first Symposium here in Maine. I've talked to some of them and have listened to their stories about the fear and apprehension many of them felt at that first gathering. I certainly remember the same sensations when I went to my first gay meetings—the fear of being discovered, the claustrophobia of being in a room with *only* gay men and lesbians, the sense that some irrevocable decision had been made by casting my lot with these people, that some line had been crossed that could never be denied.

After a while those emotions passed and a sense of exhilaration took over. Our coming out as a group—a communal coming to our senses—seemed the victory in and of itself.

We've learned that the world was not satisfied. It would not accept defeat in its attempts to wreak havoc on our souls. It went on to do its ravaging with our lives.

The examples of the struggles we faced ranged from the intimately devastating to the publicly lethal. Lesbian mothers were denied their children. Gay men were denied their careers. Families rejected their offspring. Communities exiled their citizens.

We didn't have to leave Maine to find that violence. It's right here. It's on the beaches of Ogunquit and on the streets of Portland. All we had to do was listen to the members of the state House of Representatives when, during their debate of a bill to grant us minimal civil rights, they likened our morality to that of barnyard animals. These acts of violence are not random events. They are part and parcel of a pervasive hatred directed at all of us.

Most of us hoped that coming out would bring us peace of

mind, but instead we find ourselves forced to be defiant and always on alert. We have each fought so hard to assert our own sense of self in a world that denies us, and we would like to luxuriate in our new-found individuality, but we can't. We can't because the world will not allow us the extravagance of a peaceful, individual existence separated from the violence around us. We have been obliged to learn the full meaning of Hannah Arendt's words: "When you are attacked as a Jew, you have got to fight back *as a Jew*. You cannot say, 'Excuse me, I am not a Jew, I am a human being.'"

We cannot ignore the basic fact that the hatred directed at gay people *anywhere* is directed at us as well. Just as we learned to hate gay people when we were closeted, so we have to learn to love them when we come to our senses. We have to acknowledge their struggles as our own battles, their defeats as our own losses. When a gay politician in San Francisco is assassinated, it is an act of violence against all of us. When a machine gun is fired into a gay bar in New York City, we are all the intended victims.

We have not *chosen* to lead our lives this way. We don't *want* to listen to the right wing describe us as animals. We don't *want* to wonder if the merchants of Ogunquit are talking about us when they say they don't want "that kind" in their precious village. We don't *want* to have to constantly examine every candidate for every office to make sure we aren't electing officials who think we're slime.

But we must. We must, because we cannot escape our connection with one another. Just as we have taken self-hatred and worked our magical alchemy to produce pride, so have we taken society's shunning of us as a group and transformed a hated population into a valued community.

It is vital that we all understand what has occurred in the past ten years. It's important that we understand our history and the context of our lives. It is even more essential today than it was a year ago. It is essential because gay men are now facing a crisis of such proportions that we just may lose everything we have gained in the last decade. There is a new havoc being wrought on our souls and our lives, and we have got to face it squarely and intelligently and courageously.

The mysterious and frightening epidemic labeled AIDS is spreading unprecedented panic across the country. It is making us scared of one another, suspicious of one another, and it is leading us to make unforgivable judgments on one another.

AIDS *is* horrifying. Whatever you've heard about the disease, let me tell you this: it's worse. However confused you are about its origins, let me tell you this: the medical community probably knows less about it.

The only relevant fact about AIDS is this: gay men are the first victims.

In their excitement and well-founded need to alert us all to the danger of AIDS, the media and most of the gay leadership and medical establishment have spoken to us with great agitation. They thought they had to scare the bejesus out of us to make us pay attention. They've done their job well. I don't know a single gay man who isn't aware of this epidemic.

I want to bring into balance one effect of AIDS that's too often left out. I want to talk about the victims and how we treat them.

I can't speak dispassionately about this subject. I've just returned from New York, where I spent time with a former lover who was diagnosed a year ago as having AIDS. I am concerned for him and about the way the gay community and the medical establishment are responding to him.

In our panicked response to AIDS we have been all too quick to blame the victim for his disease. We want him to have done something wrong to deserve what's happened to him and to convince ourselves that it couldn't happen to us. In the face of the irrationality of AIDS, we've become desperate to find cause and effect at work. But there is not a single statement anyone can make about AIDS that will stand up as a truth.

Do you think all people with AIDS were wildly promiscuous? You're wrong.

Do you think they all used drugs? You're wrong.

Do you think they all live in New York and San Francisco? You're wrong.

Do you think they were already unhealthy? You're wrong.

Do you think you are invulnerable because you aren't like them, whatever that means? You are very, very wrong.

Because many people believe these easy generalizations, there has been an obscene undercurrent of thought that the victims are somehow the causes of their own illness. No one deserves a disease that is probably terminal. No one seeks out an infection that might lead to a particularly virulent cancer.

We're told that parts of our lifestyles might increase our susceptibility to AIDS. We're told what not to do, or what to stop doing, or what to cut back on. All the wording makes it sound as though anyone who does contract AIDS has asked for it. This certainly isn't true of the men who are suffering the disease now. They hadn't this information years ago when they became infected.

People like Billy, my friend, lived their lives as best they could. They attempted as much integrity and—granted—enjoyment as they thought possible. Now they have AIDS. The media—gay and straight—usually tell us about their plight in the most academic and distant terms. I want to personalize this for you and tell you just what's happening to Billy. Billy's temperature has not dropped below a hundred degrees in over a year. He cannot go past two o'clock in the afternoon—on a good day—without needing to sleep because of exhaustion. A simple common cold will force him to stay flat on his back for two weeks. Billy has been defiantly self-sufficient since his seventeenth birthday. Now, at the age of thirty-one, he hasn't the energy to work, nor can he keep any coherent schedule because of the omnipresent possibility of becoming sick. Once a successful commercial artist, he now survives on welfare.

When he wakes, the first thing he has to do is check all his body surfaces for topical infections. Any one of them might represent a terminal disease.

Billy has to face every day filled with this reality of death. There's no way he can avoid it. He belongs to an AIDS support group, ten or so men who gather together regularly to talk and nurture one another. In one week—*one week*—one member of Billy's support group died and three were hospitalized.

What has anyone done to help him?

Many of his friends have deserted him. They are frightened of his disease and refuse to stay close to anyone whose death may be imminent.

Gay groups have raised money for research about AIDS, but there is no fund, not even in New York City, to help Billy with his day-to-day survival.

Only recently have any real numbers of gay men in the city been willing to go to the victims' houses and help them with the most elemental chores that they often are too sick to perform themselves.

I want you to know what it's like to have AIDS and to listen to the medical establishment:

When Billy first recovered from the shock of hearing his diagnosis he decided to educate himself as much as he could. He went to a panel discussion where the first speaker gleefully described the research opportunities AIDS presented as "a great moment for science."

What Billy wanted during all this time was someone to hold him—just once in a while. He wanted some physical contact. But whenever he told someone he had AIDS, or when he approached his friends who already knew, he was almost always rejected.

In our ignorance we are losing our senses. In our fear we are losing the ability to remember that we have become a community that needs to care for its members. Our panic is leaving our most vulnerable members isolated and alone. Many gay activists are horrified by the specter of a disease spreading through the community. Some doctors and some gay men are calling for isolation of all gay men exhibiting symptoms of AIDS. If you want to be nice, you call these leper colonies. If you want to be real, you call them concentration camps.

While men like Billy have to face a daily fight for their lives, they are also forced to react continually to the ignorance of the world around them. While they should be cared for by us, they have to watch and weigh our words to make sure we are not going to abandon them utterly. We must not.

We have every right and every obligation to examine every opportunity to combat this disease. We have no right to desert the men who have already contracted it. We have every obligation to demand that they receive the best care, the most human convalescence, and that they are treated with dignity. If we let ourselves or the medical establishment treat these men as though they are lepers with "bad blood," then we are accepting a heinous definition of ourselves. Just as we could not allow the psychiatric establishment to rule us "sick," so we cannot allow anyone to tell us these men deserve their fate.

All the AIDS activities and organizations have a real and important place in the fight against the disease, but I see some of them a little differently than you might.

Usually AIDS education is directed at telling you how to avoid the disease. But I want you to be educated because I want each of us to have worked through the shit and fear before we have to deal with a friend or neighbor or lover when he comes down with it. The chances that some states will never have any native cases of AIDS are nil. We are not dealing with the question "Will AIDS come to Maine?"; we are dealing with the question "When?" And when it happens that some man in our community is diagnosed as having AIDS, I don't want that person to be treated as a leper. I don't want him to be shunted aside and ignored and feared by the rest of us. I want us to react to him in the best way we can. I want us to have already come to our senses about this disease and be able to respond as a compassionate community.

We need to promote AIDS research. We must do everything possible to find a cure. But every time you give to this cause I want you to ask why it's our burden to pay the cost. In May of 1983 the federal government allocated less than $250,000 for AIDS research. That same day President Reagan requested an additional $110 million to fight a war in Central America. How dare the government price our lives so cheaply! And how dare you let them! There is no excuse for any gay person not to write to every senator and member of the House and demand emergency funding for this crisis.

And before you talk about research, remember the human dimension of this tragedy. The victims, most of whom were hard-working, self-accepting gay men, now are paupers, dependent on Medicaid and welfare. We must care for them somehow.

If we allow our own fear to let us deny our connection with people who are facing death, we make a mockery of our attempt at a communal existence. If we can stand up and declare ourselves proud to be gay, we must also show some substance to our gayness. Our lives have been testaments that we will not allow the world to trivialize us. We have insisted that being gay is more than a sexual act. We have demanded that the world— and we ourselves—see gayness as a way of being, of relating, of loving. Now, faced with a monumental crisis, we are being challenged as we've never been challenged before. We have to respond with righteous anger, careful caution, thorough preparation, and, above all, complete compassion.

We must be angry with the medical establishment that would reduce the suffering of gay men to an opportunity for exotic research. We are not curiosities. We are people who need a dramatic response to a serious health crisis.

We must be angry at the political establishment that would try to buy off our health needs with token grants.

We must be cautious that we don't panic. We have to remember we are facing an incomprehensible disease, and we must not go off believing every untested theory or improbable hypothesis. We must be guarded against those people—gay or straight—who overtly or covertly suggest that this or any other disease is the appropriate result of being gay.

We must prepare ourselves with as much knowledge as we can about AIDS, and we must insist that our public health agencies, our government, and our doctors and hospitals prepare themselves for the possibility of the disease showing up anywhere.

And we must be compassionate. Men who are sitting beside you in a restaurant or sunning with you on a beach, men who stand beside you in a bar or dance with you at a disco may become victims. So might you. Your friends. Your lovers. Your brothers. When that happens these men are going to experience a havoc wrought on their souls unlike anything they have yet known. They are going to need your support and your caring.

They do not need your fear, your ignorance, your panic.

Billy looked me in the face when I was in New York and told me he was going to live. No one should have to fight that battle alone.

1983

In Residence at the AIDS Project

———————

Believing firmly in the healing power of telling his own stories, Preston
wanted to facilitate the process for others. He created the position of
writer-in-residence at the AIDS Project of Southern Maine, where he
helped Mainers with AIDS document their lives. The following two essays reflect on that experience.

———————

I had been trained and had worked in the sexual health program at the University of Minnesota Medical School. I had the
background, then, to comprehend what was happening from
the beginning of the AIDS epidemic. I had been a happy par-
ticipant in the sexual revolution, and I understood that those
activities meant I was at risk to contract the disease. None of
that cool, careful, distant knowledge prepared me for the moment when I actually heard my own diagnosis. A frigid wall
came down, separating myself from my emotions, from my
family and community, from what might be going on with myself and my body.

My wintry detachment lasted for two years. During that
time I went through untold numbers of treatments and consul-
tations with different physicians, becoming professional in my
ability to report my medical history to a new doctor in a con-
cise and practical manner. That doesn't mean I became any
more competent in my ability to handle the disease.

Through those two years, I lived in a context of so much death that war is the only metaphor I can use to describe the experience. I received sometimes daily reports from people around the country. Ben was sick in LA; Patrick was dying in Seattle; Kris had passed away in Sante Fe; Vito died in New York.

Here in Maine the numbers began to add up. The names changed, the friendships might have been different, but death was all around me and it was only getting closer.

It became, finally, a necessity that I write about AIDS. A few stories and articles appearing in different media had moved me with their ability to articulate what was happening. I had clandestinely clipped them and kept them in a folder. I could barely bring myself to open it up and read these essays and narratives. They burnt me.

Eventually I brought them together with some new work I'd asked other writers to prepare, and with my own writing, and published them as an anthology, *Personal Dispatches: Writers Confront AIDS*.

I found more than relief in that accomplishment. I found liberation by facing down the disease that apparently was eating me away. I found strength in naming the truth. My writing was certainly emancipating. After having stopped all but a little journalistic work for two years, I was able to go back to my real vocation, the creation of books.

I am an activist by history. Whether it was the civil rights movement in the 1960s or the antiwar and gay and feminist movements that followed, I was accustomed to taking part in the action of society. It was not strange that I had taken part in establishing the AIDS organizations here in Maine, and in working on AIDS projects across the country. I knew I wanted to share the kind of empowerment I'd experienced with both the clients of the AIDS Project and others with HIV infections.

I wasn't then an officer of the AIDS Project, but I knew the people involved and we agreed to create a writer-in-residence program with two components. First, I would expand my work taking oral histories of gay men in Maine to include some who were living with the disease. Second, I would establish a process whereby those with HIV infections in Maine could work with me on their own writing, and I would help them present their work in published form to the Maine reading public. Similar programs had worked in other areas. At San Francisco State University a program published the creative work of people living with AIDS, and in New York novelist John Weir had chaired a writers' group for Gay Men's Health Crisis, the oldest and largest AIDS organization in the country.

While I used these programs as models, I knew I had to be careful to listen to people in Maine. Even as I approached the Maine Arts Commission to fund the writer-in-residence program, I made sure that whatever we agreed to do would be something that fit the needs of the clients.

Still, I had some expectations I know were shared by the staffs of the AIDS Project and the Maine Arts Commission. My own experience had been that of a professional writer turning to his art to cope with the frightening experience of living with a probably terminal diagnosis. Art, however we might define it, comes from that kind of experience—at least that's what we writers and others who are schooled in the liberal arts would like to believe.

I've worked with at least twenty people in Maine since the writer-in-residence program began. Although not all that much "art" has been produced, in no way do I believe the program a failure. Far from it. It's been an unqualified success, but in ways none of us had anticipated.

The media, aided by some elements of the AIDS movement, portrayed those who had the disease at the start of the epidemic as highly valued members of society, even though they were gay. It's not just that the general populace was first made aware of the disease by the death of movie star Rock Hudson; the names that made the headlines were those of powerful lawyers and politicians, clothing designers and novelists. We were, the media told us, losing people vital to the arts in America. The deaths of black and Hispanic people, especially drug-users and single mothers, weren't important enough for television and tabloid attention.

Maine is one of those places where the media image's lie about the person with AIDS takes on particular meaning. Although in this state people with the disease are indeed gay men (though numbers in other groups are growing), these men are not wealthy stars with grieving fans.

One of the first men with whom I worked was a guy from Lewiston who felt his pending loss of life sharply. It was unfair that he should die now, he told me, because he had finally gotten a warehouse job with a salary of over five dollars an hour. It wasn't *fair*, he used to cry, that he would die at this moment of success. His weren't the standards of a Perry Ellis, but his story was just as important. This man's story is precisely the kind recorded by my oral histories. As I've taken my tape recorder around the state and listened to people's life stories, I've been most struck by the extent to which people are convinced they aren't important enough to be listened to. Who would care? What value would anyone find in the life of a waiter or a warehouse worker or a fisherman? Then, with the tape recorder running, the most dramatic and powerful stories would come out of these men. Here were novels of trust and betrayal, legends of reconciliation and the discovery of peace; poems of love and happiness.

I hope these oral histories, and others I've taken from gay men in Maine over the previous five years, will eventually be published as a book, if for no other reason than to convey to my storytellers that their words have been recorded. As the great Lord Chesterfield once said, "Many a man would rather you heard his story than granted his request."

The larger part of the artist-in-residence program feeds into that same promise, that same hope. I did not discover many

nascent poets among the clients of the Project. I found no un-
discovered talent that will wow them in New York, or even in
Orono. I did discover people who were desperate to have their
stories told and who were sure no one would listen.

I had thought my grief about AIDS was the most intense
sorrow I could feel, but I found new levels of heartache as I
learned how utterly unvalued people in our society think they
are. For many of those I worked with, the program functioned
to give them the courage to write letters to the daily newspaper
in their hometown. They hadn't felt they had a right to petition their neighbors in those columns, or they were frightened
that they would look foolish if they used their limited education to construct a letter. They wanted someone to go over
their writing with them, to make sure they wouldn't be made
buffoons.

And there was another heartbreak in the work. Almost all
writers I know have some aspiration that their work will outlive
them, that their words will be a trace in the sands, allowing
them to live on in the minds of future readers. I was unpre-
pared, though, to learn just how primal that ambition is.

From the very beginning, people have sought out the program to ask for help in writing letters to be delivered after they
die. One man wanted to write a letter to his mother, forgiving
her for not coming to his bedside when he was sick. "She's going to feel so bad when it really hits her," he told me. He
wanted to offer her absolution. Another wanted to leave a letter for his lover, telling him how much the lover's care and patience had meant as the man had sunk further and further into
feebleness. Still another man wanted letters sent to certain politicians, who he blamed for not caring enough about his and
his compatriots' situation. "They should know that a person
died because of what they did!" he screamed.

As I've worked with each of these people, helping them ac-
complish just what he or she desired, my life has been affected
by theirs. I was not a distant "helper" but one of them. Their

concerns and their insights have informed me and changed my own work, driving me toward different goals than those I might have had, relieving me of my own isolation just as my work relieved them of theirs.

What we were doing more than anything else was affirming one another's importance. The Maine Arts Commission might have wanted publishable work to come out of this grant. I haven't delivered that. But I've delivered something as important, I now realize; I've delivered a sense of worth to people who hadn't experienced it before and who, when faced with their own death, needed it more than ever.

1991

AIDS Writing

This essay was originally delivered as a speech to the plenary session of OutWrite, the first national lesbian and gay writers conference, held in March 1990.

John Updike has complained that today's writers are losing relevance. "The modern writer, perceiving that his reach is not wide, hopes that it is high. Priestly longings cling to writer-consciousness—pre–Vatican II priests, who kept their backs to the congregation while chanting in Latin." According to Updike the writer is no longer connected with real life; the writer is indulging in his or her own world, incapable or even disdainful of reaching out to connect with what is happening in the reader's reality.

Nowhere is that disconnection more obvious than in the stories of AIDS. As I approach what's going on in my world, I find that the doctrines of contemporary literature and the taste of the current publishing scene simply cannot tolerate AIDS writing that's meaningful.

One of the volunteers who works with the writer-in-residence program at the AIDS Project in my hometown of Portland, Maine, tells about his work with one of our clients, a man in the terminal stages of the disease. The client wanted to leave behind a series of letters for his son. He asked the volunteer to take his dictation; he was too ill to do the writing himself. The letters were to be left behind to be opened at certain significant moments of the son's life. There was a letter for the day of his First Communion, another for his entrance into high school, one for graduation. The list went on. The purpose, so simply stated, was to give the son actual proof of how much his father loved him. The father was beset with grief that he would not witness these markers of his son's progression into adulthood. He wanted the boy to pass those markers with evidence that the man who had been his father cared for him and, even from the grave, was with him at those moments.

The story is the kind of anecdote I tell groups when I want to describe the utter humanity of people who are living with HIV infections and who face death. It always works—how could it not? But there's a kicker to the story. Just as everyone in the audience has taken it in and tried to reconcile its emotion, perhaps dismissing it to bathos, I add another fact: The father was nineteen years old at the time.

That's the problem with writing about AIDS. The emotions are too raw. And the scale is too great. Modern writing tends to want controlled feeling that has a narrow scope. Tom Wolfe has written in *Harper's* that the American novel has lost touch with the story of American life. To Wolfe, the contemporary writer is willing to settle for too small a stage; today's novelist ignores the epics of our daily life and retreats inward, avoiding the sweeping narratives moving all around.

The story of the young father proves Wolfe's point. It is only one of many examples of life in the time of AIDS that would be easily and contemptuously dismissed by critics and publishers alike. The narrator's appeal to what would be called the reader's most base sentiments would keep such a story from ever being accepted by our critical establishment. The argument that it is *true* would have no standing.

But the true stories of AIDS in our world, in our country, in my home state of Maine, are too large to stand the confinement of the current critical canon. This is another story about AIDS in Maine:

One of the first people I knew with AIDS was a man who bred dogs. His constant companion was Martha, the bitch who gave birth to all the others and who had been with him for years. The man, originally from Georgia, still had a southern drawl. He and I used to stand in bars and watch televised college football games together. He followed his University of Georgia Bulldogs with a passion matched only by his love for Martha.

None of us was used to AIDS when he became sick. We hadn't yet learned how to cope with young men dying, handsome men becoming ugly with damage, their muscular bodies whittled down to stick figures by the wasting of the disease. We did not ignore him. We took him to the hospital. We made sure he kept his doctors' appointments. We visited him. But we didn't know how to talk to him about this strange and frightening illness. We didn't know how to discuss his coming death, even among ourselves. We joined him in a process of communal denial. He wasn't really in danger, we agreed with him. This was just a passing discomfort, we said. There was really nothing to worry about.

We kept up that pretense even through the last time he was able to come home from the hospital. When we helped our friend into his house, Martha heard the doors opening and closing and the sounds of our voices. She ran from the back of the house, running to greet her master as she had done countless times in the years before. She cavorted toward us and we all laughed, waiting for her to jump up on us. But she stopped in midrun, in the middle of the living room floor. She froze. Then she fell back on her stomach, cramping her legs beneath her. She began to move backward, away from us and her master. A loud, mournful, keening cry came from deep inside her. She had seen death in the lesions that covered his now emaciated body.

And so the defenses of a whole group of adult men were destroyed by a dog's honesty. We all wept then. The forced laughter was gone, shown to be the lie we had all known it to be. We sat down and we held our friend while he cried, finally able to confront what was going on.

Use that in a novel and see what an editor says. Put that in a short story and watch your work dismissed as overly emotional. What's more, take a dozen of these stories—and every gay man has them, many other people are going to have them in the future—and you will be dismissed as an hysteric.

That a contemporary person could witness dozens of deaths in a single year and do it in the face of ignorance and bigotry, and also be forced to cope with the possibility that his own death will become one of the statistics, is a story of such breadth that modern writing cannot contain it. This story has to be dismissed, because horror at these narratives isn't something that the dogma of contemporary writing can accommodate.

Do you think this is all too much? That I'm still only pulling strings? I have known, literally, hundreds of men who have been infected with HIV; I have known, literally, dozens who are dead. I am forty-five. I am also the oldest of us all. I live in a time that offends nature, a time when the old are burying the young. How can that be written about in any way that doesn't sound like a bizarre comic book contrivance? How does this become part of our story?

What does it mean to our writing? Now, to me, it means that the purpose of AIDS writing has to be found outside of any conventions that contemporary criticism and publishing might try to impose. The canons are proven ineffective, inappropriate. What is "literature" becomes a meaningless academic question when what is defined can't accommodate what is happening in our lives. What is happening to us because of AIDS is too great for modern writing to measure. That's not the fault of AIDS; that's the limitation of modern writing.

Those of us who are writing about AIDS can't worry about these definitions any more. We can't be concerned with careerism, with academic acceptance, or with having the fashions of the day dictate how we write. We must not be worried about the styles and trends of a real or perceived literary establishment. We can't use AIDS to enter doors of a house that can't or won't entertain our issues.

The purpose of AIDS writing now is to get it all down. Andrew Holleran says the purpose of the writer in the time of AIDS is to bear witness. Sarah Schulman makes the case that we cannot allow ourselves to be separated from what's happening by being seduced into an observer status. To live in a time of AIDS and to understand what is going on is to know that writing must be accompanied by action. Writing is not what our teachers told us, something that stands alone.

To be a writer in the time of AIDS is to be a truth-teller. The truth is more horrible than anything people want to hear. The truth is that millions of people in the world are dying of a disease that could be controlled. The truth is that care is not reaching people who need it. The truth is not the comfortable television movie of the family reconciled with the victim. The truth is homeless young people wandering our cities without a national health care program. The truth is hundreds of thousands of women in Africa dying because they've never been educated about risk reduction and because they live in a society that makes women chattel, torsos to be used by men without concern. The truth is devastating. The truth can't be contained in a pleasantly structured short story that will satisfy the readers of a literary magazine.

We have to *get it all down*. All we can expect of our writing that does get published is that it create the historic documents that might make sense to people in the future. That's all published AIDS writing can hope to be today.

In our writer-in-residence in program, I've learned another important function of the writer in this time of AIDS. I had thought we'd find art in our work, helping our clients become like Updike's priests. Isn't there the romantic notion that literature comes from suffering? How much more suffering can there be than that experienced by people with AIDS?

But there was no art, not in that sense. There was need. I have ended up transcribing thoughts and emotions. I began with the story of the father who wanted to leave letters for his son. That kind of work is the unexpected major function of my project. I take dictation from clients who are furious with the media and politicians. We help our clients write letters to family members, forgiving them for never having come to the soon-to-be-dead person's hospital bed. "My mother will feel so bad when it finally hits her," one man told me. I write letters of thanks for people who want their loved ones to know their help and patience were needed, welcomed, adored by those who received them.

So far away from being a modern-day priest who tries to reach high, I find myself brought back down to earth. I am instead a scribe in the marketplace of a society where literacy is so rare it has become a profession. I have become not the author of the story, but the means for telling the story, the tool used by people to let the world, their families, their friends, understand what is going on.

This is the best writing I can do in a time of AIDS.

1990

A Woman of a Certain Age

About two months before he died, I was in Preston's hospital room at Maine Medical Center. Somebody knocked on the door and I went to see who it was; Preston was leery of visitors. I opened the door and saw a tiny woman, no more than five feet tall, with a halo of perfectly white hair. I had read "A Woman of a Certain Age," and I knew before she said a word that this must be Franny Peabody.

In the worst of his illness, Peabody visited Preston nearly every day, first in his hospital room and then at his apartment. She was always cheerful but never falsely so. She was equally at ease with Preston's mother (at seventy, her closest peer) as with his twentysomething adopted gay "nephews."

Franny Peabody recently endowed an AIDS hospice in Portland called Peabody House. When Preston died, Peabody House was one of the charitable organizations to which donations were designated. It was a fitting, if extremely sad, last chapter to their remarkable friendship.

Franny Peabody turned ninety in 1993. The party for her was a bit unusual. To fit in all her friends, the celebration had to be held in the atrium of One City Center, a major downtown office building cum shopping center. A mountain of small cupcakes was handed out by volunteers—a single cake would have been impossibly big for the size of the crowd.

But these aspects of the celebration were just outsized variations on the standard theme. The real hint of how exceptional this ninetieth birthday party was came when the Maine Gay

Men's Chorus led the crowd in a rousing, very gay rendition of "Happy Birthday."

I was one of the people who gave toasts to Franny that day. When one knows a person like Franny, delivering testimonials is part of the program.

Franny's grandson Peter died of AIDS early in the epidemic. When he was ill and wasting away, Franny and her daughter Barbara (who wrote about the experience in the book *The Screaming Room*) discovered that they were dealing with mass hysteria and mob ignorance along with medical tragedy. Franny decided that the loneliness and the social ostracism her family had experienced shouldn't be the norm. She was determined to do something about it.

The little AIDS work going on in Maine was very low-key. Back then, AIDS looked like an urban disease to many people, something that only happened to gay men and drug users living in major metropolitan areas. Still, one AIDS support group met in the basement of First Parish Unitarian Church in Portland. I belonged to another organization, the Maine Health Foundation, which met in people's homes. Neither group had been activated yet because no cases of AIDS had been diagnosed in Maine. But we knew the cases were coming, and various clusters of us were getting ready for the onslaught.

AIDS wasn't a chic disease in 1986, it was a frightening one. But here, into the basement room of the downtown church, walked Mrs. Millard S. Peabody, the great matriarch of Portland society.

Franny was used to volunteer organizations. She'd been on the board of directors (often as president) of the Portland Museum of Art, the Maine Historical Society, the Portland Landmarks Committee, the Colonial Dames of America, and many more.

The members of the AIDS support group weren't used to

having society ladies in their midst. They were grassroots activists, committed to egalitarianism. They had no idea what to do with Franny.

She told the story of her grandson and announced her intention to do something about the need for education, and the need for the compassion which she was convinced would come from that education. And with that first visit, Franny took the nearly invisible movement of AIDS activism in Maine and made it instantly respectable. That's the power of a Yankee woman of a certain age and standing in the community.

The church-basement support group eventually evolved into the AIDS Project of Southern Maine, the major service provider for people with AIDS in northern New England. Franny spoke frequently on behalf of the AIDS Project about the need for more education and funding. She gave countless interviews to the media. We were out to stop the disease, nothing less, and Franny was going to be our Joan of Arc.

Her family was shocked by her activities. Her daughter Barbara has told me that Franny was one of the most puritanical mothers possible, one who kept a tight rein on her children while they were growing up. Now, here she was, a great-grandmother, carrying bags of condoms to rural schools and distributing them, even giving little lectures on how they should be used. "I can't believe that's *my mother*!" Barbara said.

Franny had access to places—like those rural schools—where the rest of us could never go, at least not so easily. School administrators were cautious about letting gay men into their buildings (who knows what we would do to their young pupils?). But Franny was everybody's grandmother. She was so white-haired charming, and so well known in the community (and was rumored to be *so rich*—though she's always denied this), that no one was about to block her entry into any institution.

Franny had other access as well, into areas that we gay men who had been doing all the AIDS work didn't always understand. Once the epidemic hit Maine—and it hit hard, when it came—she made a special ministry of meeting with the parents and grandparents of the men who had the disease. She was there, driving all around the state when it was necessary.

The parents she counseled were often being struck by a double revelation: not only were they learning that their child had AIDS and was going to die, but for many they were just now discovering their child was gay. Franny had a unique authority to help them navigate these difficult waters. She had been through the same things herself.

Her son Scotty, who lives on Long Island, is gay. Few people in Portland knew this until Franny disclosed it in an interview with a national newsmagazine. (Scotty claims to be the only gay man in America who's been outed by his mother in the pages of *Newsweek*.) Scotty's initial coming out had not been particularly smooth, but he and Franny had worked through their problems and Franny had come to accept fully her son's gayness.

As a young mother, Franny had nursed all her babies through what at that point was the most horrible epidemic of modern American life—polio. She knew what it was like to sit helplessly and watch a child come close to death. She knew what it was like to learn a son is gay. She knew what it was like to lose a grandson to AIDS.

Eventually, she began support groups specifically aimed at relatives and friends of people with AIDS. Franny, who is so elegant it sometimes hurts, is one of the last people you'd ever expect to see facilitating a support group. But she did it all the time, sitting on pillows on the floor, dressed in her impeccable matron's dresses (*never* in a pair of slacks, please!) and a string of pearls around her neck.

No conversation is out of bounds for Franny. I remember one of the first times I was with her during a group discussion. The topic was AIDS and the arts. The question was just how badly the arts in America were being hurt by the disease, as it was carrying off so many creative people in our society. Some of the members of the group were uncomfortable with the sub-text of the conversation. Aren't all deaths equal? Isn't it some-how elitist to separate out certain people as being more im-portant than others?

Franny listened to it all and nodded her head in agreement with many points of view. She didn't seem to be especially con-cerned about the idea of elitism, though. "My dears, *of course* AIDS is hurting our culture. Of course it is! Just go to New York and walk down Fifth Avenue. There hasn't been a decent window design in years!"

I spent a lot of time with Franny, especially after our volunteer efforts merged and I joined the board of directors of the AIDS Project. I became the president, and she was the guiding spirit. The cost of AIDS care in Maine skyrocketed in the late eight-ies as more and more cases were registered and more and more people required care. (Also, it turned out our health care sys-tem was markedly better than most, so we experienced a major influx of people with AIDS from other states—people who wanted access to our hospitals and specialists and to the com-passion that seemed more abundant here than in neighboring New Hampshire or Boston or New York City.)

The pressures mounted and the AIDS Project faced bank-ruptcy. Franny convened a luncheon meeting in the Cumber-land Club, the bastion of Portland's ruling circles. She strong-armed a dozen of the most powerful people in the city to come: the head of the local newspaper, a television station manager, the chairman of the board of one of the biggest banks. When all the power brokers had been seated, Franny addressed her peers: "My dears, I did not order the lobster roll," she told them, "because it was too expensive. I saved money on the menu, and I intend to give that money to the AIDS Project. Now, let's see what the rest of you are going to do."

For the first time in my life, I witnessed the instantaneous mobilization of a charity. Pledges were made, committees were formed, lists of contacts written. Franny oversaw it all, making sure the waitresses kept the wine glasses full. ("It does help to have a touch of the grape, you know, my dear," she whispered to me, "it loosens them up quite a bit.")

Enthusiastic with the luncheon's success, we arranged for the most obvious method of raising lots of money quickly: we would give a dinner in honor of Franny herself. Just as the movers and shakers had come to her luncheon, there was little doubt they could get their wealthy friends to a party for Franny. Who in Portland society would dare *not* attend, even if the charity was AIDS?

As the date for the dinner approached, there wasn't a hint of anxiety on Franny's part, except her concern about how much money would be raised. It would have been indelicate for her to browbeat people into attending a dinner in her honor, but that didn't keep her from getting us to do it for her. "Now call the Smythes and make sure they're going to be in town," she'd instruct. "After all, Jean Gannett Hawley is flying back from Florida just for this event. Certainly the Smythes can make the effort not to be up at the lake that day." Franny's motivation had nothing to do with ego; she could have cared less if people wanted to pay tribute to her. But she was counting on the ticket sales.

It was a grand event, in the largest ballroom in the state. The governor and his wife, U.S. Congresswoman Olympia Snowe, shared the head table with me and Franny and a few assorted dignitaries. The mayor spoke and there were greetings from every imaginable group.

In some other cities, when there were social events to raise money for AIDS, the organizers would often duck the "gay issue." To take part in AIDS fundraising, they assured the benefactors, did not mean you had to accept gay lifestyles. You could buy your roast beef at these benefits and never have to hear the word "homosexual." Franny didn't let anyone get away with that at her dinner. "Didn't the gay boys do a wonderful job with the flowers?" Franny asked all the (paying) guests as they arrived.

That dinner was the first of many times I've spoken at a celebration for Franny. My speech was a disaster. I cried through the whole thing. I hadn't realized just how much I loved Franny before I gave that talk about her work in hospitals, the way she would sit with young men and their families, bringing pots of tea and finger sandwiches to whomever was hungry. I realized as I delivered the speech that I trusted Franny to be sitting by that bed for me when I became ill.

When I finally got through the talk and sat down, the governor gave me a manly handshake; Olympia Snowe congratulated me on a powerful speech; Franny kissed my cheek.

Franny has always had a sense of priorities. As a part of the dinner, Republicans in the state had arranged for President Bush to name Franny a "Point of Light." When the White House telephoned for a presidential chat about the honor, Franny refused the call. She claims she was just too busy to be kept on the phone that long, but I think she just didn't want to talk to Bush. Franny had spent much of her life as an Episcopalian, Republican shoe factory owner. Now she was a Unitarian, Democratic AIDS activist. She didn't think somebody like Bush, from her old world, could understand.

We received so much money that night that we not only saved the AIDS Project from financial ruin, we were able to establish a small endowment fund with some of the proceeds.

There were times when Franny's worlds would collide, or threaten to. She was once given an honorary degree by the University of New England Medical School (not the only one she's received, believe me). A problem developed: the school was at the same time bestowing an honorary degree on Secretary of Health and Human Services Louis Sullivan, archenemy of the grassroots AIDS activists. ACT UP planned to disrupt the ceremony.

Franny was distraught. She wasn't about to give up her degree, but she didn't want her attendance at the event to be misinterpreted by her activist allies. Beyond that, a public protest just seemed like such bad manners.

I was Franny's escort for the ceremony. When we arrived at the auditorium there were dozens of ACT UP members sprawled all over the entranceways conducting a "die in." Franny and I simply stepped over peoples' bodies. "Hello, Frank," she said to one pseudo-corpse. "Lovely day."

"Same to you, Franny!" the protester called back.

Then grandmother Franny showed her colors. "My dears, are you getting cold on the ground?"

"We're all right, Franny," the activists answered.

We waved and gestured our way through the demonstration with all the grace we could muster, accepting the fashion queens' compliments on Franny's new frock, purchased especially for the commencement.

I don't remember ever actually telling Franny that I had AIDS, but she found out. Our relationship became more complex as I was not only a fellow activist and counselor, but now a counselee as well. Franny began taking me to frequent lunches, stage directing every one of the dates at the Cumberland Club or the Portland Yacht Club or in the dinning room of a big downtown hotel. She actually wasn't so concerned about the stylishness of the dining establishments as she was with the noise level.

Franny's hearing has been failing, and if there was too much noise in a room she could not follow a conversation. I often caught her smiling blankly at people who were talking in a din. Franny's loss of hearing and her frustrating experiences with hearing aids were one vehicle she had used to reach out to people with HIV. Here was her own example of a failing body, here was the place where she suffered the agony of knowing she was facing death in a short period of time.

When the last man who had been my lover died, I called Franny and asked her to lunch. She must have caught something in my tone of voice, because she cleared her schedule immediately, so we could get together that day.

I was in some place that seemed beyond depression. George had been my companion from my earliest gay days, the witness to more of my gay life than any other person. I had other friends, many of them. And certainly there was a large gay community that I could count on. But with George's death, nobody remained from *my* era, my original circle.

Franny is seldom very emotional. She is, after all, a Yankee matriarch. This one time there were tears in her eyes. "My dear, it's so horrible," she said. "All *my* friends have died as well."

She saw that I didn't quite understand, and continued: "You see, my dear, all the people I know now are the children— sometimes the grandchildren—of the people I knew when I was young. The ones who are my own age are gone. I'm left calling sixty-year-old women 'girls,' and I sit and feel so alone some times. This is what you must be feeling."

"And a sense of guilt," I added.

"Yes, I know that as well. Why me? Why me, indeed? What happened that this one life has gone on when others were cut short? There's a desperate desire to have this all be rational, but it's not. It's just how it happens. That doesn't end the feelings, though. Not at all. Those go on, those feelings of loss and abandonment. I suppose there's a great joy in living the extra life that you and I have both had, but there's also the fear that it will go on too long, isn't there? The danger of lingering when one's body is incapable of sustaining one.

"I find myself just hoping that the end comes quickly,

cleanly. That I don't have to spend untold years in a nursing home, unable to care for myself.

"At least I am no longer frightened of death," she said firmly. Then she took my hand. "That's the one thing you young men have given me. You have shown me that one can die with dignity and with courage. I was so petrified of death, it was so frightening, but now I understand that death comes, that one can greet it with a sense of propriety. I've sat with so many men and watched life leave them. So many, and they were all so brave. You will be, too. You already are."

We sat quietly for a moment. Then Franny sat up to her full (inconsiderable) height and smiled. "And, now, my dear, how about a cocktail?"

1993

Living with AIDS, 1992

Even after compiling *Personal Dispatches: Writers Confront AIDS*, and after working as writer-in-residence at the AIDS Project, Preston struggled with how to write about his own fight with AIDS.

"Living with AIDS, 1992," was his most profound attempt to document and make sense of his illness. The piece was the first chapter of an AIDS memoir Preston planned to write. As with so many other projects, the book itself became a casualty of the disease.

I woke up one morning in May of 1991 with excruciating pain. It was so strong that it made any movement impossible. I tried to imagine where this torment had come from. I couldn't figure it out. I decided that it would have to pass, or at least it would have to lessen; nothing this acute could continue to exist. I stayed frozen on my bed and waited for some relief. None came.

I finally struggled to reach my phone, only a foot from my bed. It took at least five minutes to will myself to stretch my arm and torso far enough to pick up the receiver and dial Amanda's number on the touch-tone pad.

"I think something's very wrong. Can you come over?" I rasped out when she was on the line. "I think I'm in trouble."

I couldn't have hidden the tension in my voice if I'd wanted to. I could hear her concern as she assured me she was on the way.

I had to get up out of the bed and cross into the living room to reach the buzzer that would let her into the apartment building. I couldn't stand. I slid onto the floor, then crawled the ten feet to the intercom. I was exhausted by the time I got there, absolutely drained. I propped my body up against the wall, sitting on the floor, and waited for the bell to ring. I think I passed out from the exertion, but the buzzer woke me up. I took minutes to get upright enough to press the button that would let her into the building.

Amanda didn't take any time to ask many questions once she was inside. It seemed obvious that a heart attack was what was probably going on. The pain was centered in my chest; I couldn't breathe; my color was ashen. She called 911 and quickly went about trying to make me comfortable. It was foolish, but my main concern was having strangers find me in my underwear—I certainly hadn't gotten dressed and couldn't. Amanda went into my closet and got out a robe.

Things work in Portland, Maine. There wasn't that long, impossible wait for help that one hears about in bigger cities. The emergency team was at my door in minutes, less time than it had taken me to drag myself across the floor.

I can barely remember the EMTs. There was a man and a woman. They were noticeably efficient. They were also very calm. We spent a lot of time trying to find a position for me that was comfortable, but it never worked. Even while they were trying to put me at ease, an oxygen mask was snapped onto my face. Then they carefully and gently said the words, this might be my heart. A nitroglycerin tablet was put under my tongue. A portable monitor was strapped to my body. I looked so terrible that no one was going to wait for any results. I was going to the emergency room at Maine Medical Center, and I was going there *right now.*

Some of my fellow tenants were in the hallway as I was carried down the stairs and out the building to the waiting ambulance. They expressed concern, told Amanda to call to let them know what was happening. I couldn't have responded to them if I'd wanted to. I was still paralyzed by the pain.

It was only as the ambulance was screaming its way to the hospital that the woman medic, who was in the back with me, announced that it wasn't my heart after all; the EKG showed nothing. That didn't mean anyone slowed down. Whatever was making me sick was making me very sick and there was no dearth of concern among the four of us about that.

I was hurried into the emergency room. The medics yelled out the results of the tests they'd been able to perform on the way. Doctors were called, nurses and attendants moved over to lift me off the stretcher and onto a bed. Amanda stood by, worried, waiting, wondering what to do. I couldn't help her. I couldn't do anything but exist on that bed with my pain.

More oxygen, more monitoring equipment, more tests—all of them STAT—right now. The doctors seemed to become more calm as they read their machinery and interpreted the data it was sending out on computer screens. No, this wasn't my heart. I had no fever. There was something wrong, but this wasn't an emergency after all.

I was hardly conscious, but I remember feeling like a fool. This was going to end up being an unexpected anxiety attack of some kind. I was going to be humiliated for having caused all this trouble.

There was one very important problem, though. I wasn't getting enough oxygen into my system, even with the mask forcing me to breathe directly from the tank. There is a small and intriguing piece of equipment they have now. Without breaking the skin, they simply attach it to your finger and it reads the level of oxygen through your skin. In one of the many incongruities of that day, I ended up being fascinated by that piece of modern technology and, when I talked, it was the one thing I wanted to ask about.

Amanda was busying herself, making calls. Tom was on his way, incredulous, she said, since he'd seen me the night before

and I'd been in great shape. What could possibly have happened?

There was action all around me. Only a few of the patients
were given privacy by a thin cloth drape; most of us were pur-
posely visible to people in the nursing station in the center of
the emergency room. I kept on looking at the scene with a kind
of dispassion. I had worried for years that I might be making a
mistake by staying in Maine after I knew about my infection.
Perhaps I needed to be closer to Massachusetts General Hospital in Boston or some other major research institution. Were
the health care facilities in Maine going to be good enough to
provide what I needed?

I looked around at the activity in the emergency room and
found some satisfaction; indeed, this was a fine hospital. I
laughed about caring that I was in a decent medical center,
even while all the rest of it was going on around me.

Doctors—medical students, interns, residents of various
kinds—kept coming over and reading my chart, wondering
what could be going on. Nurses kept on reading my oxygen
level. When one of them touched my hand to apply the device
to my finger she said, "Wait a minute."

I had a fever. It had come from out of nowhere. Now everyone went into action again. "He has to breathe," a doctor said
and ordered a morphine drip. There was a calm, authoritative
voice explaining that the pain was keeping me from drawing in
enough breath. With the fever, they couldn't count on the ache
being alleviated. The morphine drip would help.

The very word "morphine" was the most terrifying thing I'd
heard so far. I'd sat deathwatch with many people and I knew
morphine is often what comes last. The doctors use it when
their medicines no longer work, when the only thing left is to
make the patient "comfortable." I watched, fascinated, as the
IV was set up by my bed and the needle forced into my veins. I
was on morphine. This was serious. Any doubts about a simple
anxiety attack left my mind.

But the morphine didn't touch the pain. The pain had ceased to be anything that could be described as "intense," "excruciating." The pain had transcended those definitions. It had become a noise that was so all-consuming that nothing else could be heard. I could only take small photographic looks at the nursing station, the concern on Amanda's face, the flurry of activity around me.

The pain was devouring my consciousness. It wouldn't let any other message into my mind.

I couldn't even become concerned as I listened to the hospital staff rush around discussing me. They had a term for me: I was a patient who was "crashing and burning." I still couldn't breathe; my fever continued to climb.

Someone finally removed the IV, but not to take away the morphine. "We can't wait for the morphine to work in solution, we need to give you a direct injection. Pure morphine will burn while it goes into your system," the nurse said as she took a needle and drove it into my vein.

Tom had arrived and stood by the bed, promising that Robert had been called in New York, asking if Anne should be called in New Orleans. What else should be done? He had with him a medical power of attorney, giving him the right to take control of all these procedures if I couldn't do it. It was something we'd agreed to months ago.

I couldn't respond to much of what he was saying. Only a few thoughts could come into my mind. One was the ironic realization that I had spent four years waiting to die and now that it was going to happen, I couldn't even pay attention. I was being eaten by the pain, still, always. The noise it caused continued to drown out everything.

X-rays were taken, more blood was drawn for more tests. I was moved to a room upstairs; Tom and Amanda took care of the admissions office. Even the many doses of morphine couldn't mask the hurt when my body was jostled about by the attendants. I was weeping by the time I was in the bed.

My fever went up again, to over 104 degrees. More morphine was ordered. More antibiotics were ordered. Six IV tubes sprouted from my arms. I was crashing. I was burning.

Pain and drugs kept me from comprehending any passage of time. Robert arrived and stood by the bed; he'd flown up from New York. Michael and Mark were in the hallway; they must have gotten out of work. Amanda had left, not knowing what she should do, what she could do. Tom stayed, running the show.

There was a quiet gloom in all of them, and in the doctors and nurses who kept coming to my bedside. Specialists were called in; pulmonary specialists, critical care specialists, infectious disease specialists went through their lists of questions and prodding. They finally agreed there was nothing more that could be done for me even if I were moved to intensive care, but if my breathing didn't improve soon, emergency procedures would have to be taken. An opening in my throat, a respirator, something had to be done to stop my crashing and burning, something had to be done to let me breathe.

Tom and Robert spent the night. Tom was desperate to do something and began to keep cold cloths on my forehead. They seemed to heat up and dry out as soon as they touched me. He kept rotating the cloths, using them to fight the fever; at least that part of the problem should be able to go away.

Sometime before dawn the fever began to drop. Once it started, it fell rapidly, moving away from the brink just before the deadline the doctors had set for more emergency procedures. The level of oxygen began to rise. The relief on the face of the intern who'd orchestrated my care the last hours was obvious. I was going to make it.

The next few days were a blur. My parents drove up from Massachusetts in the morning. Friends and neighbors came to the hospital. I was so high on the morphine that I actually had animated conversations with some of them, or so I'm told; I hardly remember a word.

It had been a bizarre form of pneumonia, I told them. That's what the doctors had finally said. It had been a sudden and an acute attack, one that I might not have survived if I hadn't lived so close to the hospital. Hearing the doctors say "pneumonia" had been terrifying for all of us; it had the same effect as the sound of the word "morphine." Pneumocystis pneumonia is one of the most common, and at that time the most deadly, of the opportunistic infections that strike people who have an HIV infection. My friends, my family, myself, all of us were stunned by the idea that I had survived pneumonia, even if it evidently wasn't Pneumocystis. This had been the way we all expected me to die, and so my escape was all the more amazing.

I spent ten more days in the hospital. The attack had been so severe that I needed that time to recuperate. The pain hadn't disappeared when my fever broke; on the contrary, it had stayed. My system was wrecked by all the medicines that had been surging through it—my mother still talks of the horror of seeing all those IV tubes sticking in my arms. I was fed by IV for days, only getting down a minimum amount of jello or ice cream, hardly anything more solid than that.

I remember great separations from my body. The drugs were definitely the major cause of that. Morphine seemed to separate me from my earthly self. I could laugh and say that now I understood why people took heroin; the sense of rupture between my self and my mind was so complete, the escape from temporal concerns was so complete, it was no wonder people used this simple narcotic to achieve peace.

My own calm was much more complete than my jokes indicated. The doctors confirmed the worst fears we had—that I had escaped death, barely. I was still amazed that it had come so close without my being able to investigate it. Only the drugs allowed me even to contemplate what had happened; only they could turn down the volume of the pain enough to let me take in what had been going on. I had approached death and it had not frightened me. I had advanced toward the end and there was no white light, no sudden salvation, nothing. Nothing, that is, except a certain peace. The lack of fear was the most startling part of it all.

When people came to the hospital and asked me about what I'd gone through, I would tell them how the pain had made it impossible to pay attention to what was happening, how the pain had blocked out the awareness of what had been going on. But that wasn't wholly true, because the pain hadn't obstructed my awareness that I might have been dying. I knew that. And it hadn't frightened me. I was astonished by it.

None of my words could express what had really happened. I couldn't find a way to tell people that pain becomes noise, that it becomes a living thing in your being. I couldn't express the serenity of it all. I had thought I would fight endlessly to save my life, that I would be panicky at the idea of life ending. But I hadn't felt any of those things. I had instead simply been aware that death was coming close and that it might claim me. I had slipped through its hands this time.

I was told I could check out of the hospital at the end of ten days. Tom and others had been by my side the whole time, and their actions had convinced my doctors that I wouldn't be left uncared for.

I couldn't wait for anyone to come and get me, though. I was too eager to leave. I was so weak I could hardly walk, but I managed to get dressed and get by the nurses and leave on my own energy.

When I first got outside the building I thought I was still under the influence of drugs. Everything was so beautiful! I thought I might have been overcome by the entire experience and now was seeing reality through proverbial rose-colored glasses. The answer was much simpler. May is when spring turns to summer in Maine. When I'd gone into the hospital, the trees had been budding and the plants had been coming up convincingly. In those ten days inside, though, summer had arrived in full. The trees were covered with new-growth leaves and the plants had blossomed into an amazing array of colors.

I could only make it a block at a time, then I'd have to sit down and catch my breath. The stops were actually welcomed. Each one gave me an opportunity to live with the new season a bit more. This was what I loved about living, the sheer sensuality of a New England summer, the soft breeze from the ocean, the explosion of color that came out of nowhere, out of the gray and bleak landscape of winter in Maine.

We have so much water here, the climate might be tropical if the temperature were just warmer. Trees and other plants don't wither from the heat, they last the whole summer. The colors don't fade, the types of blossoms just change and bring a new palette with them everytime they do.

So this was living? I shuffled down Brattle Street, on my way to Park, where I lived, and loved the feeling of it. I actually laughed out loud at my close call.

I also told myself that I had some work to do. I had nearly died, and the thing that bothered me the most was that I hadn't been able to pay attention to it. I had experienced that sense of peace, but that was all. The pain had knocked out any other investigation or experience. Now the pain was gone, but the awareness of death wasn't. I had to go back and listen to the messages I had received in the hospital—and had received in the years leading up to it. I had to do that in order to understand what this other thing—this living—was all about.

1992

World AIDS Day Speech, 1993

The speech Preston delivered at Portland's First Parish Church in obser-
vance of World AIDS Day 1993 was his final public appearance, and one
of the very last things he wrote.

So much had changed since he first wrote about the disease in "Some
of Us Are Dying," but the essential message remains almost identical:
AIDS is the responsibility of us all, because "We cannot define our community as only the few who look like us, act like us, love like us."

It's the first of December. It won't be long before we have the
first big snowstorm of the season—you probably think of it as
something you've escaped this year, since we all know it could
have happened by now.

There's a great peace when those storms blanket the city.
The peace comes from the quiet. The noise of urban life is
subdued. All of us find the comfort of isolation.

But December first is also the day when we acknowledge
AIDS. The timing is too appropriate, because we have come
to act with regard to AIDS as though a snowstorm is going
on—a time of silence and isolation.

In the past few years we have allowed AIDS to become expected. It is simply something that is happening to a few
people. After all, most of the poster boys you came to recognize here in Maine—all those pleasant young men who asked
for compassion—have died now. Maybe you think that's it, that

there are no more such nice young men to care about. The new people with AIDS are as unlike most of you as were the gay men from New York who were first shown on television more than ten years ago, with their open sores and frightened gazes. They're so angry, confused, and impolite. You can separate them from our lives.

But your choice would be a violation of being a New Englander. It would be a violation of the idea that we are members of a New England community.

Sure, we congregate on a single day of the year and make soft sounds. We run in marathons. We have come to believe that this is enough; we have done our duty. AIDS has become something as commonplace as heart disease or cancer, just one of those bad things that happen to people.

We cannot continue to give in to this deadly virus. It continues to spread through our population; it is poised to devastate Thailand, India, and much of the rest of Asia as it continues to ravage Africa. It is our responsibility to make noise in the face of this disaster. It is our responsibility because we have no right to define our New England community by our concept of today's style or self-important self-selection. We cannot define our community as only the few who look like us, act like us, love like us.

When the first snow falls, we have to think of the people who will be left out on the street, not just those who are in comfortable apartment buildings or houses. It is our imperative as ethical human beings to identify with them.

And it is our ethical imperative to think always of the people who are going to die of this virus. Yesterday the Clinton administration finally announced the appointment of an AIDS task force. It's easy to be cynical about the proclamation that the secretary of Health and Human Services made, that there would be a new initiative to find a cure and a vaccination and implement new preventive measures. But who's going to make sure that this happens? Who's going to let the administration know that we care whether homeless people, single mothers, drug users, gay men, and other disenfranchised people are important to them?

We have all collaborated in a silence that will never communicate those concerns to Washington—or to Augusta, even to city hall. We're all guilty of having withdrawn from the battle. We have abdicated our communal responsibility by hiring social workers and other surrogates to do the dirty work, and by believing that we have no other obligation to deal with people with AIDS.

We cannot continue this conspiracy of silence.

Perhaps the issue is simple—that AIDS represents an overwhelming barrier, that it's too big to get a handle on, that it's too much for us to think we can influence its course. This notion in itself is a collusion with the silence. We have to believe and act as though we are agents in this world.

So you can't work in a laboratory and find a cure? You can make sure the government understands that you care if a cure is found. You can write your representatives in Congress. You can telegram Secretary Shalala and let her know you're watching to make sure she follows through on her promises.

Maine will enter into a statewide election as soon as the holidays are over. You can make sure that every candidate in every debate at every point in all the primaries and during the general election addresses AIDS. You can insist that no one be allowed to leave the podium without making a pledge to do something to stop the spread of AIDS.

What you can do—in so many ways—is to end the growing silence. You can wear a red ribbon and be prepared to tell people why you are doing it. You can stand up in a school committee meeting and ask why the schools don't have a sufficient AIDS curriculum. If you're a student, you can ask why there aren't more AIDS-related materials on your reading lists. If you're a teacher, you can ask your administrators why there aren't more educational publications on AIDS available. When your employer or your corporation draws up its list of charities, you can make sure everyone knows that someone in your company cares if AIDS is one of the priorities. You can stop someone on the street who you know is active in AIDS work and say thank you. You can write to that friend of a friend who you know has AIDS and say you're thinking of him or her. You can wonder what social service agencies are doing and ask for specifics. You can insist that bureaucracies be accountable; after all, you are a citizen—they work for you. You can answer every time a religious bigot says that people with AIDS deserve to die. You can talk about AIDS in front of the children. You can insist on bringing up the conversation at a party. You can take the risk of being perceived as a fanatic. What else is there to do but be a fanatic in the face of a tragedy as big as AIDS?

When you walk into a bar and don't see condoms being distributed, you can ask the manager why. You can ask your dentist if he or she treats HIV-infected patients and under what conditions. You can ask your physician if he or she has AIDS patients or would accept an AIDS patient in her or his practice.

You can write the State Department and demand to know how much foreign aid is directed toward the disease. You can write the editor of your newspaper and ask what coverage they're planning. You can complain because coverage of World AIDS Day hasn't been a bigger priority on your television station. You can ask your friends how they're allocating their charitable donations this year. When you send your own checks, you can ask the organization how much of your money goes to AIDS work. You can ask why people are hushed when they talk about someone who has died of AIDS. When you see an ACT UP demonstration, you can join it. Yell out loud and be angry.

If you are a poet, dedicate your work to those who are dead and those who are dying. If you are a musician, perform at a memorial service. If you are a visual artist, paint the horror, sculpt the madness. If you are an intellectual, envision the devastation and describe it to everyone who will listen. If you are a minister, preach the gospel. If you pray to a god, ask forgiveness and offer up the names of those who have passed on.

What you can do—what you must do at every opportunity—is break the silence. You can stop this cover of silence from falling on people with AIDS. You can insist that AIDS is not something that should be expected. It is not something we should concede to. It is not something anyone should be quiet about. You can listen to the voice of every person with AIDS who rants and raves about the treatment he or she is receiving from cold bureaucracies or uncaring organizations. And you can amplify those cries as loud as your own voice will allow. You can make a difference. If you speak, then you will be doing your part in helping the fight against this horrible plague.

From the start of this epidemic, every AIDS activist has intuitively known one thing: Silence equals death. It's up to you to decide whether that nightmare will continue to be true.

1993

A NEW ENGLAND CHORUS

Some writers write—or claim to—without any consideration of who might eventually read the work. They create art for art's sake, out of a need for personal expression, and the fact that others may come to observe that art is immaterial. John Preston was not one of those writers.

Preston never sat down at his writing desk without knowing exactly the group of readers he was addressing. He explained, "If I write anything, I know who I'm writing to, and anyone else who wants to listen can. But addressing that audience [is] more important than what I [am] writing."

By defining his audience as gays, or New Englanders, Preston did not intend to limit himself or to exclude others—as he said, anyone who wanted to could listen in. But he wanted to write from a place of shared traditions and common assumptions, where he didn't have to explain himself.

Preston gloried in major book contracts with New York publishers. He was proud to have been published in *Harper's* and quoted in the *New York Times*. But it was of equal or greater importance to him when he was asked to write for the *Casco Bay Weekly*, a local Portland paper, or when *Maine in Print* accepted an article. He was exceedingly pleased with the final interview he gave, to *Preview!*, a small biweekly Maine paper.

Preston was confident of his place in the community of lesbians and gay men; after all, he had helped create some of its earliest institutions. But if he could maintain his gay identity and at the same time be accepted by what he called the "New England chorus," he knew his life had achieved completion.

This section includes two essays about Preston's sense of connection with his audience, and a final piece encompassing the entire scope of his personal journey: acceptance, expulsion, wandering, and acceptance once again.

A Minister Calls

I am not a good housekeeper at all, but for some reason I had been compelled to clean up that day. I had washed the floors, dusted the mantels, polished the furniture, washed the windows. My home was unusually sparkly. After I'd taken a shower to wash the grime off myself, I continued in my new homemaker role and made banana bread.

Just as I was taking the bread out of the oven, enjoying the sweet overripe steam of a fresh loaf, the doorbell rang. It was the minister of the nearby Unitarian fellowship.

Now it's not often that a minister shows up unannounced at my door. As a gay man, I have developed an instinctive distrust of men of the cloth; official religion doesn't usually bode well for us. This particular minister was a vague acquaintance. We'd been on committees together doing AIDS work and lobbying the state legislature to pass a gay rights bill.

It seemed a bit presumptuous for him to show up unannounced like this, but a clean apartment was such an event for me that I was thrilled to have a witness. I invited him in and made a pot of tea. We sat down at my gleaming dining room table, where I hoped he would notice the two freshly burnished silver-plate candlesticks.

My guest was famous in town as the radical minister, the one who could always be counted on to show up at peace demonstrations. He had been one of the first and most ferocious protesters in New England to speak out against the Vietnam War. His horror at armed conflict did not fade when the United States left Vietnam. He used to picket the shipyard that was built in Portland in the late 1980s, even though it was one of the city's major employers. He didn't care how much the economy was hurting; he didn't want death machines being manufactured in Portland.

After a few bites of hot bread, the minister came quickly to his point. He had come to see me, he said, because he wanted to know more about my thoughts on gay life. He had been impressed by my articulateness when we were lobbying the legislature, and he wanted to hear in depth my perceptions of being gay in Maine and in general.

It wasn't that I was the only gay man he could talk to. The minister had gay members of his congregation; everyone in the city knew it was one of the houses of worship where lesbians and gay men were most welcome. But he must have seen me on a different level. I was a native New Englander, so I wasn't a complete outsider, but my political skills and intellectual pretensions had been polished in Chicago, Minneapolis, California, and New York. There weren't many gay activists living in Maine in the 1980s who were as adamant about politics as I was.

We talked for a while, and then I sent him on his way with copies of my articles and essays on gay rights, inviting him to come back in a few days to discuss his reactions.

The visits became fairly regular over time. My apartment was never as clean again as it had been that first visit, but the minister didn't seem to mind. He would show up at my apartment door and I'd make a pot of tea and we'd sit at my dining room table and discuss the latest article or speech I'd written. I started to show him my writing before I sent it off to be published, using his critiques to guide my revisions. He became my most careful reader.

I was amused when the minister discovered some of the erotica I'd written. He seemed agitated by it, very interested in talking about it. I thought it was because my writing pornography made me seem less respectable in his eyes, made my political writing somehow suspect. But the minister treated my erotic work with the same level of seriousness with which he scrutinized my polemics. He found important themes in my dirty books—many more, in fact, than I'd ever intended to put there. I realized he was struggling with the question of what gay relationships should look like. He seemed amazed that my portrayals of chance encounters often depicted characters who dealt with one another decently, that there seemed to be meaningful relationships even in some of the anonymous sexual couplings I wrote about.

The minister began to tell me that I was like the men and women of his denomination who had been so active in social change during the nineteenth century, when Unitarians had led the way in the abolition and feminist movements. These early activists had understood that one has to bring the arguments in favor of justice directly to the people, he told me. He admitted that there was a good bit of nostalgia in his comparison. He was thinking about an era when a congregation's attention and loyalty could make its pastor one of the most influential persons in a community. That the church can seem so peripheral in modern times frustrated the minister; he wanted to find a way to make it a center of authority and inspiration once again.

One day, during our regular visit, he announced that I was the person who would help him revitalize the church. It struck me as ludicrous at first. After all, I was a leader in the gay sexual revolution, a large part of which had been concerned with shedding the oppressive connections to organized religion. But the minister explained that his congregants were really struggling with my issues in their daily lives—how to be gay in an ethical way in society. What we should do, he declared, was set up a series of lectures in the great Unitarian and Universalist churches of New England. I would speak on such topics as the ethics of gay politics: Were gay issues so pressing that they should be given attention equal to issues of racial equality?

How should gay men relate to their families? Who was obliged to do what for whom? Was silence about one's sexual identity something that society had the right to expect, or was the personal cost of being silent too high to pay?

I would be like a modern-day Emerson or Thoreau, the deep thinkers who had gone from one Protestant cathedral to another speaking to the people. I would develop each of the topics into a specific lecture which I would deliver in one of those great buildings—in Concord, Massachusetts; Concord, New Hampshire; Montpelier, Vermont; Boston. When the circuit was completed, I would publish the lectures in a book. This, the minister assured me, was to be my great contribution to society.

The minister's plan fed every bit of ego I had. I was completely swept up in the idea, certain that this was my calling. My self-perception is intimately tied to New England, and I was all too aware of the great intellectual and literary tradition I would be stepping into. This was my big chance to make the ideas of the gay revolution part of the intellectual history of New England.

I began to plan out the lectures, honing the topics and devising ways to ensure maximum media exposure. I put in long hours outlining my thoughts, typing up abstracts of speech ideas. My speaking tour of New England became my top priority.

Without warning, just as I was moving into full swing on our joint project, the minister stopped coming by. The first time, I convinced myself he had just gotten waylaid by some business at the fellowship, maybe a congregant with a family emergency who needed counseling. I kept on baking loaves of banana bread, expecting he'd show the next time. But the loaves grew stale and began to mold.

A couple of months later I discovered that he'd come out of

the closet, left his wife of twenty years, resigned his position, and was last seen marching in a gay pride parade in Cincinnati, Ohio.

What had happened, of course, was simple: he had used me. He had used our conversations as a form of counseling. He had known gay people before me, but they were his parishioners, so he didn't feel comfortable going to them for support. But I was not in his congregation. I was safe.

I became extremely angry when I thought about it. He'd been completely dishonest, just like so many other hidden homosexuals who leech the strength from those of us who are out, who take our passion, our ideas, and our lives and then use them for their own private benefit. Throughout our supposed friendship, the minister had been the intellectual equivalent of the man who stays home with his wife except for occasional visits to a male prostitute, to whom he would give only money—never emotions, never fidelity. I was forced to question the sincerity of his every word and action.

My anger was intensified because I was acutely embarrassed by my own behavior. A writer's greatest crime is self-aggrandizement. And I had been caught naked with my dreams of being one with Emerson and Thoreau. How could I have dared?

With time, my feelings about the whole encounter evened out. After all, I realized I had achieved a goal of sorts by showing another gay man that it was possible to lead an ethical and fulfilling life as an open gay. It took me a long while, but eventually I came to hope that the minister had parted with his wife with some gentleness, that he had found a place for himself, and that he had achieved some peace.

I also realized that there was a lesson for myself in this episode. It occurred to me when I was asked to speak at the Lesbian and Gay Community Center in New York. The building is a renovated schoolhouse on a side street in Greenwich Village. It's ramshackle and could use some paint, but it houses an amazing number of exciting activities.

On this occasion I was speaking at an event sponsored by the Publishing Triangle, a professional organization for gay men and lesbians who work in the publishing industry. The audience was large and appreciative. I had addressed similar audiences many times before. I'd spoken to the Gerber/Hart Archives in Chicago, an organization devoted to collecting gay history. I'd spoken to a gay and lesbian lawyers' group, and another time to an organization of bar owners. The venues were often less than luxurious—basements and backrooms are typical meeting spots for grassroots organizations—but the gatherings had been vibrant, alive with the exchange of information and opinion, just as I imagined the cathedrals of medieval Europe.

In Portland I had been so wrapped up in my relationship with the minister because he had promised to give me access to the great churches of New England. But now I realized I already had access to the people I really wanted and needed to address. The people in the Lesbian and Gay Community Center, the lawyers and bar owners, all the people who read my regular columns in gay newspapers—*they* were my congregation. I didn't need to be in Old South Church to reach my audience.

Writing has always been a conversation for me. I have always known that lesbians and gay men were the people to whom I am speaking. But I've never thought our conversation had to be private or limited in any way to the gay community. I've always hoped that others would overhear what was being said. I suppose this is the quest for the universal that writers and critics talk about, the desire for everyone to be able to relate to what is put down on the page. But the universal has to begin with the specific.

My specific writing has been directed to lesbians and gay

men. It has been about the realities of our lives that most people don't want to recognize, and it has been about people even the gay world ignores.

I am the son of a working-class New England family that has always taught me to struggle with questions of fairness, social justice, and heritage. I have been part of a gay generation that has included men who have been shot, men who have killed in self-defense, men who have been murdered for no other reason than that their appearance was "too gay," people who have been ostracized and abandoned to a plague of epic proportions.

It has been my work to document what we have gone through, not only so it can be remembered, but so we ourselves can examine it. What does it mean for people to live in the mill towns of Maine and lose their jobs and have their lives threatened because they're homosexual? Where are our connections? What is happening to us now that AIDS has infiltrated our tentative hold on a place in society?

The minister who used to visit me may have suggested the grand lecture tour merely as a ruse. It was a trick, a way of keeping me interested so that he could spend time with an openly gay man, gathering strength from my example until he had the courage to come out himself. But in the end, he was right. These are the great issues for our community, and they deserve to be heard. Maybe not in the old churches of New England, maybe not from the ancient podiums where Emerson and Thoreau once stood. But in the community centers, the bars, the bookstores, the small magazines and newsletters— there we will be heard.

1993

Winter Writing

I read at Now Voyager, the lesbian and gay bookstore in Provincetown, on a Thanksgiving weekend. I had been on tour for nearly two months: San Francisco, San Diego, Los Angeles, Seattle, Chicago, some other places in the Midwest—I can't really distinguish them in my memory any more. The visit to Now Voyager was the end of the last leg of the travel. I had driven down to Massachusetts and signed and read books along the way to Cape Cod. Until that afternoon in Provincetown it had all been a chore, something I had to get through.

I had been interviewed in endless hotel rooms and eaten lots of bad food. I had traveled so much that I began to feel as though airplanes were places where people lived rather than a form of transportation. The main purpose of a book tour is to present the author as a commodity, to have the writer interviewed and collect publicity. I was good at it, charming to interviewers (most of the time), and I had done a good job; my publicist told me so. But there hadn't been much time to spend with readers, and even when I had read to an audience I felt I was on stage, a performer more than an author. I entertained people, but I hadn't connected with them. I had not had the powerful experience of reading out loud to an audience and receiving a strong and immediate reaction to my writing.

My favorite season is winter. Here in Maine the days are short and the light is obscure. The cold encourages me, and everyone else, to stay inside. A silence envelops the apartment, especially when it snows—snow stifles noise, it makes it easier to concentrate.

I spend whole days talking to no one but my animals, the

dog and two cats. These are the only companions I can tolerate while a novel or a collection is being put into shape.

Solitude is so necessary for my writing that I sometimes forget it needs to be broken. The crowd at Now Voyager helped me relearn that.

When I began my reading, I started with the obvious selections—my own essays from my most recent anthologies, the handsome books published by the mainstream publishers paying for this tour.

There were small murmurs in the room as I read—sounds of agreement and recognition that energized me, made me aware of the muscularity of at least some of my writing. The sounds of the audience were barely whispered affirmations. I had told a story with which my peers, my friends, my readers could identify.

I became a writer because I wanted to capture the stories that had helped me create my identity. Many of those stories took place in Provincetown, the place where I learned most of my lessons about what it meant to be a gay man in my native New England. My first book, *Franny, the Queen of Provincetown*, and many of my first short stories came from my experiences in that resort village.

I hadn't planned on doing so, but I began to read *Franny* to the audience. We obviously shared at least the experience of Provincetown and the ancient queens and dykes of the village who had been the rebellious pioneers of our culture. There seemed a sweet solidarity in the room as I read the stories of my youthful vacations on Cape Cod.

This reaction from the audience, this sense that we were sharing what I had written about, was, I realized, the real reason I tour and read. Of course I'm after publicity. What's the use of creating all these words if no one knows they're available? But more than that, I wanted the sense of connection with the audience. I had spent my hibernations creating words for us, using the quiet of a Maine winter to silence the intruding noises and to focus my skill as a writer. Now, being the scribe of a community, I came out from the isolation and shared the stories with the tribe.

This is not to impugn my writing. I am not a cipher who only articulates some communal statement. If I succeed, if any writer does, it has to be with an understanding of W. H. Auden: "The reader responds to second-rate literature by saying, 'That's just the way I always felt.' But first-rate literature makes one say, 'Until now, I never knew how I felt. Thanks to this experience, I shall never feel the same way again.'"

But this dynamic doesn't work unless there's an audience. Simply to express oneself to oneself isn't being a writer. There needs to be some response, some assurance to the author that what he or she has to say is worthwhile. Alone, in my apartment in Portland, I can create the words, but I can't have proof of the audience. That's what the people in Provincetown gave me last Thanksgiving weekend. For a single hour we were together in the stories I had created, stories we had all experienced and were able to reexperience through my words.

Reading in public fills many authors with fear. I understand that. There is always the possibility that no one will show up, or that only one or two people will, and the humiliation of rejection will be worse because it will be public. Some writers hate the idea of reading aloud what they had intended to have read in private. But for me, to have an audience is a vital element in being a writer. I have to leave the separation of my single life and move into the world, to listen to people and to watch them respond to my words. I need the strength that the gathering gives me to return to my words, to get them in a form to take them out again, on paper or aloud, when the winter is over.

1993

A New England Chorus

"John! How long ago was it that you lived upstairs?"

"Thirteen years, Bob."

"Thirteen years!" Bob the barber turns to the men who sit on the plastic seats and waves his scissors in the air. "Thirteen years ago, that's when I had the shop up on Fore Street. He lived up there, on the top floor of the building."

The men look at me, say nothing, and nod, almost as one. The message Bob the barber is sending has little to do with my living arrangements. Bob is telling them that I've been around for a while.

I take my seat in one of the chairs and pick up the paper. Bob never has the *Boston Globe*, it's always the *Herald*: this is tabloid territory. Conversation isn't expected, but there's an open invitation to anyone who wants to join in on Bob's constant commentary on international affairs, local politics, architecture. In this way a barbershop reflects the finest New England institution, the town meeting. Everyone is a citizen in a barbershop. Everyone has the right to his opinion.

Sometimes Bob does want a comment from a specific person. "You see that new library over by the university, John? What's with that?" He's talking about a warehouse on the campus of the University of Southern Maine that's been redone in a slightly modern fashion. Panels of painted metal make up the facade, not very traditional for a New England school.

"Should have been brick," I answer.

Bob sighs, "That's it, John. I knew you'd know what the problem was." I see a couple of heads in motion up and down the line of chairs. I am supposed to know this kind of thing. After all, I'm the writer in the group. That makes me an expert on art of all kinds. That I am an artist apparently is more important to these men than the fact that I write about gay themes.

From the beginning, my writing has presented something of a problem for people in Portland. For one thing, when I moved here I was best known for a pornographic novel I had written, *Mr. Benson*, which had achieved cult status. I also wrote adamant gay activist essays and a novel, *Franny, the Queen of Provincetown*, about homosexual characters who fought back when they were oppressed. These weren't themes that worked well in a small New England city in the early 1980s. I sometimes felt like I was outsized, I was talking about things no one here wanted to listen to.

But many of my new neighbors took a certain pride in the fact that I wrote and that I was quoted in the national press. Whenever I was mentioned in such national media as the *New York Times*, people were excited about the publicity, even if they weren't sure what it meant to have me saying those things about gay life here in Portland. Most wanted to avoid the erotica, however; we seemed to pretend I didn't really write that. Once the *New York Times Book Review* quoted me on the meaning and function of pornography. When the article was published, however, no one in Portland mentioned it for the longest while. Finally a lawyer I know puffed up his chest in preparation for some battle and brought himself to say, "Provocative quote in the *Times*, John." That was about it.

I wonder sometimes if, when I'm not around, other men don't say something like, "He's a queer writer, but he's *our* queer writer."

I finally move up to Bob's chair. He gathers a cloth around me and asks, "You want a trim, John?"

I pat my nearly bald head and ask, as I have a dozen times before, "What's the option, Bob? You going to style it?"

The men who sit in the seats laugh out loud at that. They like a good dose of self-deprecation. But I know that and I work it. I know these men. They are not a fixed set of individuals; their membership changes all the time. They are the men who hang out in barbershops. I could also find them in a local bar. They are the men who work behind the counter at the post office. They speak with a certain clarity; I have come to think of them as my chorus.

I like Bob and his shop, but actually I moved out of this neighborhood years ago. Now I live on the West End of town. When I moved I changed barbers; Norm is my man now. I did it the way you might change a parish church. But nostalgia brings me back to Bob's every once in a while, and we go through our dance the same way we first did thirteen years ago.

The discussion at both Bob's and Norm's is familiar. It's the conversation among men that I grew up with. I listen to the talk at a New England barbershop today and I instantly remember my father and his father talking about sports. Not only was this the way they could be close to one another, but it was the way that they, as New England men, shared a culture.

It's also the smells. I love the odor of the cheap bay rum at Bob's, the talc powder at Norm's. They bring back memories of being a boy, of a time when my life was simple. I was a kid who belonged in my hometown. Generations of my mother's family had lived there. No one questioned whether I was part of the community.

The barbershop in Medfield was the first place I remember my father taking me, just the two of us. It was a Saturday ritual. The men of the house, both of us, would climb into the car and drive to the center of town. We'd walk into Alfredo's and we'd be greeted by name, recognized by everyone, and we'd take our places in the chairs that lined the wall to wait our turn. I had the sense, even when I was quite young, that this was the way life went, that fathers and sons went to barbershops together and spent time gossiping and discussing the weather, that they argued about Ted Williams's batting average and got to know one another.

It takes a long time to become a member of a community in New England. Most people who move here from away think it has to do with our cold souls, ice to match the winter weather. It's just that people want to know you're going to be around for a while before they believe you belong.

I learned my lessons about New England life from my mother, a small-town Yankee who has always understood how these things work. When I was very young my parents had a small financial windfall. They used the money to fulfill the New England working-class dream: they bought a summer cottage. Theirs was on a lake in New Hampshire. My father, who'd grown up in Boston and didn't really know how the rest of New England worked, was furious that the natives kept on referring to the place by the name of the previous owners. My mother, knitting in her rocking chair on the porch, didn't even bother to look up. "It'll take them, oh, about ten years," she said. And it did.

During those ten years my father actually helped move things along. He went fishing with the owner of the local general store. Once that was done, things were easier. A local had called my father his friend, so now he had credentials. I remembered that lesson when I moved to Portland and went out of my way to be friendly with Bob in his barbershop downstairs. I knew I'd made progress when he began to sign for my UPS deliveries when I wasn't home.

You can't force this kind of thing. It has to come naturally. The men at Bob's only warmed up to me when they realized I followed sports well enough to comment on Roger Clemens's ERA and to enter into an argument about Boston College's chances for a bowl bid. I had to *know* those things and withstand a cross-examination about them. To have been caught faking it would have been deadly.

I had learned a lot about faking it. When I discovered I was homosexual, I realized that acknowledging this fact could cut me off from the community where my roots were so very deep. Who I was becoming, what I was becoming a part of, was not talked about in Medfield, certainly not at the barbershop, not even in my school, not in my family. I was becoming something that could not exist in a New England town.

I had to leave, so I chose a college as far from home as my family could tolerate, near Chicago. There I hid my sexuality, but I began by hiding my New England background.

My Yankee accent was too rough and uncultured for my college classmates. It spoke of barbershops and the working class. I didn't want to draw attention to myself—I wanted to be able to slip into the city without anyone noticing that I had gone— so I spent my freshman year in my room learning how to talk "right." Eventually I began to sound like a slightly affected voice on public television, not like a boy who had grown up in Medfield. I wanted to merge into the background and be left to find my new life in bars and clubs on the weekends.

The day-to-day existence that we gay women and men were forced into living in the sixties was intolerable. And as homosexuals across the country began to say no, we began to act out our defiance. The most famous rebellion, which started on the day of Judy Garland's funeral, was the Stonewall Riots in New York in 1969.

Suddenly, I no longer needed to live my life as a silent exile. Bands of people were marching, talking, yelling, organizing, celebrating. I began to move with the waves of gay men across the country. I moved to Boston, to Minneapolis, to Philadelphia, to New York, to San Francisco, to Los Angeles . . .

Even as I was one of those people creating a new community with a new history, I was always aware of what I had lost. I used to go to Provincetown every summer, telling myself I went there because I enjoyed carousing in the beach resort. But I came to understand I really went there because, no matter how commercial it became, no matter how many people it attracted from around the country, Provincetown was in New England. I went there every year to walk the streets and see the buildings and listen to the language that made me feel at home.

I was not going to be happy living away. I could not be satisfied with the gay life in the cities. I had to find a place where I could live with the new culture and still have a way to be a Yankee. I moved to Portland.

Not long after I moved I received my high school class's twenty-fifth reunion book. I was surprised to see that over half of us had moved to northern New England from Massachusetts. I hadn't realized I was part of any movement, but here was proof in the list of towns to which we had moved in Maine, New Hampshire, and Vermont.

I finally realized what had happened. When we were all growing up, Medfield had been a rural New England village. In the years after our graduation, however, the town became a suburb. It lost whatever was unique to a Yankee town and became more like a place you could find anywhere, say Arizona or Oklahoma. Just as I had moved to big cities in the Midwest and on both coasts after college, people with whom I'd gone to high school had tried out other regions, looking for new lives and new ideas. Still, most of us had wanted to come back to what we had known in our childhood. When we realized it could no longer be found in Medfield, we moved north.

When I went to buy a car a couple of years ago, I had more money than usual and assumed it was time for me to get a

Volvo. Isn't that what cosmopolitan men of a certain aesthetic and accomplishment drive? Volvos were cars I associated with literary types in Cambridge. They were the cars the wealthy suburbanites brought with them to Medfield when they transformed the town. They were ugly, boxy things, but they spoke of wealth and a kind of supposed good taste that would never talk about it. I went and picked one out. I even had the colors down—forest green exterior with a tan leather interior.

I couldn't write the check. To this day I doubt the salesman understands what happened, but how could I buy a Volvo and then go to the barbershop, drive to the smoke shop for my papers, be seen by my post office clerks? I went across the street and bought a black, four-door Buick Century. My artist and writer friends were aghast at the choice. "It's so bourgeois," they complained. But my New England chorus approved right away. "It'll save the family some money," my father said. "One less limo we'll have to rent for the next funeral."

"I'm a Ford man, myself," someone said at Norm's when I first parked the car in front of the barbershop, "but that Buick is a damn good car."

The chorus motioned their heads with emphatic approval and added their support with specific comments.

"Front-wheel drive."

"Solid construction."

"Buy American."

I had never admitted to any of them that I'd wanted a Volvo, but they seemed to understand it had been a possibility and immediately moved to bolster me up.

"Damn Volvos are no good in winter."

"Hell no."

"Rear-wheel drive."

"Do you know what they have to do to get those things through snow?" That brought a whole new chorus of examples of the extremes to which yuppies have to go to give a Volvo traction in a Maine winter.

"Parcels of sand."

"Bags of cement."

"I heard of one man put those big concrete bricks in the trunk and then couldn't get to his spare tire when he got a flat until he unloaded every damn one of them."

"You can't trust those people with Volvos, either," one voice insisted. "They don't know how to drive worth shit."

When the first serious snow fell that year I got the Buick, I was greeted by a wild whoop of laughter when I went into Norm's. "John! Saw your Buick going up the State Street hill the other day. You should have seen 'im," the voice said to the rest of the chorus, "that damned Buick just went right up the hill with no problem. All those little foreign cars were sliding and slipping and there was this new Volvo, couldn't make the grade, just in a little snowstorm. John just zipped right by them all."

"That Buick's a decent car," a voice said and the chorus nodded. I had made the right choice.

Sometimes the often-conflicting identities I strive for can speak together. When I went to buy a dog, I got a Vizsla, a short-haired, rust-colored pointer that impressed my neighbors in the West End, the trendy part of town. They could tell it was pedigree right away and seemed to enjoy the fact that they had to ask exactly what breed he was. I took my time to explain that Vizslas had been the hunting dogs of the Magyar nobility and had for centuries been native to the Hungarian steppe.

The noble ancestry didn't impress the men's chorus in my life, but they were impressed by the dog. One beautiful summer day I was walking him up to Longfellow Square. Most of the chorus from Norm's had moved outside and was on a bench, taking in the warm air. "Good-looking dog you got there," one of the voices said.

At that moment, as if on cue, a pigeon flew down in front of the dog, who immediately went on point. A Vizsla *is* a good-looking dog in any event, but on point . . .

The chorus gasped. It was the first time I'd ever heard that come from them, a collective loosening of the will. A voice had to explain, "That's a *fine*-looking dog." Their heads gestured assertively.

At that moment I knew I had made a perfect decision.

No matter how many books I might publish on what subjects, I am becoming one of the men in the barbershop here in Portland. They can smell me, they can see me coming. This chorus of New England men narrates an important part of my identity, and their collective voice is so strong that I have stopped fighting it. I sink into it. This is the beginning for me. I start here.

The Portland chorus's acceptance of me still can be grudging. I don't make the mistake of thinking that my sexuality is unconditionally embraced. (A joke heard at Norm's: "That one's two dollars shy of a five-dollar bill." Translation: "He's as queer as a three-dollar bill.")

I know I make it all the more difficult by being so public about my sexual identity, mentioning it whenever I'm interviewed in the media and often acting as a spokesperson at rallies or press conferences. I insist I'm making a political statement; many people in Portland have let me know they think I'm flaunting intimate details of my life which they would rather not know about.

I have friends who've been so offended by gay jokes or comments spoken at Joe's, the local smoke shop, that they've refused to go back, instead driving extra blocks to buy their newspapers. I've never heard those taunts, but there was tension when I first began going to Joe's. It used to be that when the topic of gay rights came up in front of me, the men who work at Joe's wouldn't even look me in the eye. Whenever there was a gay rights story in the local paper—an increasingly common event as the years passed—the men at Joe's would act as though I had personally wounded them.

But there are other times when the chorus comes to the defense of the local citizen. If there's someone at Norm's who doesn't know me and he starts to say something that might offend me, the chorus shuts him up. "Don't talk like that in front of John," Norm has said on more than one occasion.

Even at Norm's I'm sometimes blamed for the actions of all homosexuals. One day a wildly stereotypical gay man wearing outlandishly tight capri pants and a shirt cut to expose his midriff sauntered down Congress Street outside the barbershop. Norm looked at me with dismay and said, "Jesus, John!" as though I had picked out the guy's wardrobe myself.

In 1984 a young man named Charlie Howard was murdered in Bangor, Maine. A trio of toughs threw him off a bridge into the Kenduskeag Stream where he drowned. They did it because he looked too gay to them. I was enraged. It wasn't just that a brutal act had occurred. I was also furious that my own right to be in this place, Maine, was challenged. I took the murder personally. I knew they would have killed *me* if I had been walking down that street that night.

I moved through the streets of Portland in the subsequent weeks daring someone to hassle me. I wasn't going to let anyone take me out so casually. There was going to be a fight. There was going to be some vengeance if I was attacked the way Charlie Howard had been. I spoke with fury to any audience who would listen. I declared at a press conference that no matter what one thought about homosexuality, sexual identity didn't deserve a death sentence. That hit home to a lot of people. Violence is something that offends the truly democratic society; the town meeting only works when there are rules of conduct that everyone follows and when freedom of speech is protected. Why have a town meeting if the right to open debate is threatened with violence? The whole point is for every citizen to speak his or her piece, and that citizen cannot be expected to speak if there's danger of physical retaliation.

At Joe's, the clerk—one of Joe's many sons, grandsons, or nephews, I can never tell which is which—stared at me when I walked in the day after the press conference. I took my papers and walked to the counter to pay for them. "Heard you last night," he told me. Then he put out his hand to shake mine. "Some things have to be said, and you said them well."

My HIV diagnosis came years later. I kept it a secret for a long time. I wasn't sure how it would be handled by the chorus. I wasn't sure how it would be handled by *anyone*. I froze. At first I thought this was only my personal crisis. It was, I thought sometimes, a disease I had brought with me to Maine from away. It had nothing to do with this place. I thought about leaving, wondering if I would be better off near the medical centers of the big cities I had left.

In a short time—a very short time—I learned there were more men in Portland who had been diagnosed. I discovered that we all felt isolated. Many of them were much younger than I, and their illnesses—soon their deaths—crushed me with grief. I had somehow kept my own disease as something I could deal with; I would face it, the stoic Yankee would get through. But the sight of young men dying drove me to the limits of what I could endure. I cried. I cried often. I found myself unable to perform the most simple tasks because I would break into tears thinking about a nineteen-year-old I had seen that day, who I knew wouldn't live out the year. Or I would remember my friend who, on the last day he was alive, burst out that it was so unfair he was going to die; he had finally gotten a job that had earned him more than five dollars an hour and now he was going to lose it all.

Being isolated with these experiences and emotions inside myself became intolerable. I worked with community organizations to set up care for those of us who had the virus. I sat with men who were dying without any family to comfort them. I talked endlessly with others who had the disease. I discovered that we were a new chorus. There was strength in finding one another and in talking, even about something as seemingly inconsequential as the Red Sox.

Eventually I edited a book of essays about AIDS called *Personal Dispatches*. When it was published I did a local radio talk show and discussed the book and my own health status. The next day I went to the post office to pick up my mail. The men moved to the side and waved me over. One of them asked, "Is it true, what we heard on the radio?" Yes, I told him. There was a minute's silence and I wondered what was going to come next. "Shit, we all gotta die, John, but it must be hell to be standing on the tracks, watching the locomotive coming with your name on it."

That was all. It was enough. I sincerely thanked them for their concern and moved on.

I actually thought Norm's would be the place where I'd have the most trouble. There were all those razors and the possibility of blood, my contaminated blood that terrified so many other people.

"Got something to ask you," Norm said as soon as I walked into his shop after the word was out about my infection. He left his current customer in the chair and took some papers out of a cabinet. "The state says I got to take a correspondence course on that HIV stuff. Look through this, will you, and tell me which one you recommend."

The chorus approved.

It's spring as I write this. The baseball season is only a few weeks old. Clemens has won two games already and the Red Sox are in first place, just having won back-to-back shutouts against the Chicago White Sox. The sap's rising, and not just in the trees.

"Do you think they'll win the pennant?" some neophyte asks.

The rest of us in the chorus glare at him. It is the role of the New England man to be seduced and abandoned by the Red Sox. No matter how good they look today, it's far too early to think of such things as playoffs, let alone the World Series. The man slinks back into his chair, realizing the stupidity of what he's said.

We'll all be going through that soon enough, we all know it. The Red Sox will rise up in glory and break our hearts; they always do. It's their fate, and it's our fate to watch them do it. You can change so many things, but there are some that don't ever change. The chorus of New England men knows that; it always has.

1993

DOWN EAST

"Down East" is the New Englander's equivalent of "over the rainbow," more a state of mind than an actual location. As Preston used the term, it combines the mythology of northern New England with the mythology of gay life into a perfect fantasy.

Preston begins the following essay with the assertion that "You can never reach Down East." But the very fact that he came to write this essay, and the others in this volume, suggests that Preston came awfully close to realizing the fantasy. After a lifetime of struggling to regain the sense of belonging he'd experienced as a boy in Medfield, to find a community that would accept him both as a New Englander and as a gay man, he achieved this goal in Portland. He found—and played a significant role in building—a comfortable community.

The elusive, dreamlike "Down East" can be interpreted as a gay New Englander's take on the afterlife. I like to think that whatever else happened to him after his body ceased to function in April 1994, John Preston reached Down East.

Down East

You can never reach Down East. As soon as you arrive in a place, it can no longer be Down East. Down East must be somewhere else.

Let me explain.

Down East is a nautical term. Essentially, it's the place from where a northeast wind blows. If you are in Boston, then Down East is Maine. "I'm going to go Down East for the summer," is a statement you could make while sitting in a restaurant in Copley Square, and whomever you're speaking to—if that person is from New England or at least understands New England slang—will understand that you're going to spend the summer in Maine.

And so you arrive in Portland. And you sit in a restaurant in Longfellow Square and you tell your dining partner, "I am Down East." But you'll quickly be told that's not true, because you're in Portland and Portland is not Down East. There must be an end to this, you think. So you travel the entire length of the Maine coastline and you arrive at Eastport. "This must be Down East," you insist.

Eastport is the last town in the United States; it's the most easterly point in Maine. This must be Down East; you can't go any farther. And you sit in the diner in the middle of the village and you talk to a native and you realize that the local people know that Down East is New Brunswick, in Canada—not just the next town, but the next country.

When people think about Down East, they are not just imagining a geographic location. Because to go Down East is to go to a very different world from the one in which they live. To go to Portland from Boston is to leave behind the pressures of the city and its divisions and conflicts. Portland is Down East and that means life is easier and more slow paced and the people are friendlier and more trusting. Many Bostonians believe this, and they talk about Portland with a certain wistful expression on their faces and in their voices.

And when you're in Portland, it's no less true that Down East is a much better place to be. This city is less than a tenth the size of Boston. But it's too large for many people, and those folks have no doubt that, if they could only get Down East, they'd find a better life.

I've heard at least twelve versions of one story in the years I've lived in Maine. Each rendering is slightly different, and I'm sure there is no single source for the tale. The essentials are always the same:

There's a fishing village Down East. It's off the beaten track, and it is not one of those places that the tourists flock to in the summer. It's a small town, neither rich nor poor. It is—as all the Maine coast is—physically beautiful.

Each person who has told me the story has a different version of how he—or a friend of his who told him—happened to visit this one village. It was always the result of a small miscalculation or some other happenstance. Whatever, the man arrives in town and goes out to have a bite to eat and a drink.

There is a bar in the town. It's most often on a pier jutting out into the ocean. It almost always has a view of the colorful fishing boats that are the symbol of rough beauty in Maine. The ever-present sea gulls are flying around outside. The bar is decorated with the buoys of lobstermen and the used nets of the boatsmen. The visitor enters and is always struck by the incredible beauty of these native things, which outsiders would call crafts but the locals see only as the stuff of everyday life.

The visitor is also taken by how friendly the regular customers are. He orders a beer and is immediately brought into the conversation by his neighbors. The talk is easy and not pressured, but the visitor can't help noticing that he's a center of attention and wonders if he's intruded on some private ritual. There's some sense that he's being tested. As friendly as they are, he knows these men are trying to find out his real purpose for having come to their village. But then he suddenly understands:

The men in the bar, to his astonishment, are coming on to him. He has found the gay version of Down East. He somehow makes sure his hunch is right, and then everyone becomes even more relaxed and jovial.

The men in this bar are all—always—fishermen, with perhaps a few lumbermen or construction workers thrown in. There are no sophisticates, and the men here wouldn't know how to play arch word games even if they wanted to—which they wouldn't. These Down East men are full of good cheer and they playfully tease one another, though they'd never do that to a stranger; it might make him feel uncomfortable in their bar. They would never want to treat a guest that way.

By the end of the evening, all the men have let the newcomer know they'd like to have sex with him. But their competition to win his favor is never mean-spirited. Instead, they simply indicate that he can make a choice. Whatever happens to those not picked will be fine with all concerned (though many of the men who tell the story about this bar insist that they have ended up in a group, having sex with *all* the men who are acting so generously).

The visitor, inevitably, has to ask these wonderful men who are sitting drinking beer—and never becoming drunk—how they got here and how they live a gay life, something that straight people say isn't supposed to exist Down East.

The men only smirk. They answer, very simply, that they found one another. There are—someplace on the periphery— some women who are content with their own lives and who are happy to meet up occasionally with their legal spouses to beget children (the men in this Down East fantasy are often fathers). But the women really aren't all that interested in the rest of it. Nor are the men.

The men say they discovered one another in pairs, perhaps on fishing trips out to sea, or else as teenagers spending overnights in each other's beds. Once they were in a couple, the two men would go out together and easily joined the rest of the group. They know that this quiet life in this small village is what they really want, that these are the people with whom they want to share that existence forever.

(Along with the visitor, of course.)

They have turned this bar into their clubhouse. They come down here and meet and wait unanxiously to see if someone new might come in that night and, if he does, whether one of them will be lucky enough to get the newcomer's company and his warm body in bed.

They never leave here, they insist, because there's no reason to. One or another will talk about having been to Portland, or even Boston, and going to a gay bar. They'll all make faces at that, because the reports of those big-city places are universally negative to these men.

The urban bars are full of ugly, loud music that isn't as fine as the old standards on the antique jukebox here. The men who go to those places are always unkind, and they're rude to strangers and other innocents. They only want sex without getting to know anyone. There's no friendliness in the bars in Portland and Boston. There's only a rush to orgasm and no time to enjoy life.

The men in the bar talk about other places and ask the visitor questions about them: San Francisco and Provincetown are high on the list, as is New York. The stories about oceans of bodies on the resort beaches or crowds of gay men in Manhattan or along Castro Street certainly intrigue the men in the Down East village. But in the end they agree they don't want to go to those places, where they'd feel uncomfortable and where people would call them country bumpkins.

They have no good reason to go to the cities and suffer through that. Not so long as they have each other and the occasional stranger who'll always make sure they hear the news they need to know. They have their magazines, leftover copies of the *Advocate* and *Mandate* that somehow get to them. They're not sure what to make of the sex magazines, however; in every version of the story at least one local has a bigger one than any of the porn models, and, anyway, a cock isn't what makes a man. And the ads in the *Advocate* are written in some strange language they don't understand—what is B&D anyway?

The last statement needs an explanation. The reporters are unanimous in telling you that all the men Down East know what hot sex is like. They're fishermen, after all, and they know their knots. They're all big men and, as gentle as their emotions might be, their sex is physical. They also have great amounts of free time and one another for erotic companionship; they've had many opportunities to experiment with sex. It's just that they've never had to put names on the acts they enjoy. They have few reasons to label anything that has to do with their lives.

In the end, the visitor has a night he'll always remember and which he'll describe in vivid detail to anyone who will listen. When you talk to him, you'll see movement in his eyes, and the story's always told with the softest kind of excitement you can imagine in a man's voice. He's always going to go back there—to whatever name he's given his town. But it seems as though I always see him in Portland instead, going to the local bars and not ever showing as much inspiration as he did when he told me the story about the fishermen's bar Down East.

I've put small marks on a map of the state. Each one shows where at least one of the storytellers says this bar is. There are enough indicators now that I even think I might know the location.

I wonder, sometimes, about getting in a car and driving there. I'd like to visit these fishermen, happy and complete with their simple grasp of human nature and their open sexuality that doesn't worry about disease and doesn't understand jealousy.

The lure of the village is intense. But so is the enjoyment of the vision. If I were to go there, I might find a wonderful reality—perhaps one that's even better than what I live right now. But I would never have the dream again. And that's the risk of striving to make dreams come true, that as good as the reality might be, I can never know if it will equal the splendor of the fantasy I can hold forever.

THE COMPLETE
WORKS OF
JOHN PRESTON

FICTION

Franny, the Queen of Provincetown, 1983, 1995.
Mr. Benson, 1983, 1992.
I Once Had a Master and Other Tales of Erotic Love, 1984.
"The Mission of Alex Kane"
    Volume I: *Sweet Dreams*, 1984, 1992.
    Volume II: *Golden Years*, 1984, 1992.
    Volume III: *Deadly Lies*, 1985, 1992.
    Volume IV: *Stolen Moments*, 1986, 1993.
    Volume V: *Secret Dangers*, 1986, 1993.
    Volume VI: *Lethal Secrets*, 1987, 1993.
Entertainment for a Master, 1986.
Love of a Master, 1987.
The Heir, 1988, 1992.
In Search of a Master, 1989.
The King, 1992.
Tales from the Dark Lord, 1992.
The Arena, 1993.
Tales from the Dark Lord 2, 1994.

Edited:

Hot Living: Erotic Stories about Safer Sex, 1985.
Flesh and the Word: An Erotic Anthology, 1992.
Flesh and the Word 2: An Erotic Anthology, 1993.
Flesh and the Word 3: An Erotic Anthology, 1995.

Pseudonymous Works:

AS "MIKE MC CRAY":

Deadly Reunion, 1984.
Cold Vengeance, 1984.
The Black Palm, 1984.
Louisiana Firestorm, 1985.
The Red Man Contract, 1985.
The Death Machine Contract, 1985.
The Night of the Jaguar, 1986.
Contract: Terror Summit, 1986.
The Samurai Contract, 1987.
Blue Water Contract, 1987.
The Akbar Contract, 1987.

AS "PRESTON MAC ADAM":

African Assignment, 1985.
Arabian Assault, 1985.
Island Intrigue, 1985.

AS "JACK HILD":

Pacific Payload, 1988.
Barrabbas Creed, 1988.
Barrabbas Raid, 1988.

NONFICTION

The Big Gay Book: A Man's Survival Guide for the Nineties, 1991.
My Life as a Pornographer and Other Indecent Acts, 1993.
Hustling: A Gentleman's Guide to the Fine Art of Male Prostitution,
    1994.
Winter's Light: Reflections of a Yankee Queer, 1995.

With Frederick Brandt:

Classified Affairs: The Gay Men's Guide to the Personals, 1984.

With Glenn Swann:

Safe Sex: The Ultimate Erotic Guide, 1987.

Edited:

Personal Dispatches: Writers Confront AIDS, 1989.
Hometowns: Gay Men Write about Where They Belong, 1991.
A Member of the Family: Gay Men Write about Their Families,
　1992.
Friends and Lovers: Gay Men Write about the Families They
　Create, 1995.

Edited with Joan Nestle:

Sister and Brother: Lesbians and Gay Men Write about Their Lives
　Together, 1994.

PUBLISHING HISTORY

"The Importance of Telling Our Stories" appeared in slightly different form in *Positively Gay: New Approaches to Gay and Lesbian Life*, ed. Betty Berzon (Berkeley, Calif.: Celestial Arts, 1992).

"Medfield, Massachusetts" first appeared in *Hometowns: Gay Men Write about Where They Belong*, ed. John Preston (New York: Dutton, 1991).

"Portland, Maine: Life's Good Here" appeared in slightly different form as "Gay Life in a Small City," *Boston Phoenix*, October 1993.

Most of the "Letters from Maine" appeared in small-circulation newspapers such as *Bay Windows* (Boston, Mass.), *Front Page* (Raleigh, N.C.), and *Weekly News* (Miami, Fla.).

"Some of Us Are Dying" appeared in slightly different form as "Our People Are Dying" in *Bay Windows*, July 1983, and in *Alternative Press Annual 1984*, ed. Patricia Case (Philadelphia: Temple University Press, 1984).

"AIDS Writing" first appeared in *Taos Review*, no. 5 (1992).

"In Residence at the AIDS Project" first appeared in *Maine in Print*, vol. 6, no. 1 (February 1991).

"Winter Writing" first appeared in *Lambda Book Report*, vol. 3, no. 9 (March/April 1993).

"A New England Chorus" appeared in slightly different form in *American Identities: A Multicultural Anthology*, ed. Robert Pack and Jay Parini (Hanover, N.H.: University Press of New England, 1994).

BIOGRAPHICAL
NOTES

JOHN PRESTON was born in 1945 in Medfield, Massachusetts, and lived for many years in Portland, Maine. He was a pioneer in the early gay rights movement, cofounding Gay House, Inc., in Minneapolis—the nation's first gay community center—and editing the *Advocate*, the national gay magazine. His essays and stories appeared in nearly every gay and lesbian periodical in the country as well as in publications as diverse as *Semiotext(e)* and *Harper's*. He was the author and editor of more than twenty-five acclaimed gay books, including *Franny, the Queen of Provincetown* and the anthologies *Personal Dispatches, Hometowns, A Member of the Family, Sister and Brother,* and the *Flesh and the Word* series. He died of complications related to AIDS in April 1994.

MICHAEL LOWENTHAL is a writer and editor living in Boston. His essays, stories, and reviews have appeared in numerous anthologies, including *Men on Men 5, Sister and Brother,* and *Wrestling with the Angel,* as well as in more than twenty periodicals, including the *Advocate*, the *Boston Phoenix, Lambda Book Report,* and *Yellow Silk*. After John Preston's death, he assumed editorship of Preston's anthologies *Friends and Lovers: Gay Men Write about the Families They Create* and *Flesh and the Word 3.*

UNIVERSITY PRESS OF NEW ENGLAND publishes books under its own im-
print and is the publisher for Brandeis University Press, Dartmouth College, Mid-
dlebury College Press, University of New Hampshire, University of Rhode Island,
Tufts University, University of Vermont, Wesleyan University Press, and Salz-
burg Seminar.

LIBRARY OF CONGRESS CATALOGING-IN-PUBLICATION DATA

Preston, John.
    Winter's light : reflections of a Yankee queer / John Preston ;
edited and with an introduction by Michael Lowenthal ; foreword by
Andrew Holleran.
        p.   cm.
    ISBN 0-87451-674-9
    1. Preston, John.   2. Authors, American—20th century—Biography.
3. AIDS (Disease)—Patients—United States—Biography.   4. Gay men—
United States—Biography.   5. Portland (Me.)—Biography.
I. Lowenthal, Michael.   II. Title.
PS3566.R412Z478   1995
813'.54—dc20   94-48734
[B]
♾